Praise for *The Vanishing American Dream*

"Gene Ludwig has eloquently captured the struggle of so many American communities to realize the American dream for a new generation. In tracing the economic decline of vibrant industrial towns, he asks the hard questions about technology, globalization, the role of government, trade, our educational system, and corporations. He and the extraordinary group of assembled experts force us, with data and insightful analysis, to confront the inequality of our system. But, they also offer solutions at the local level that every businessperson, politician, and policymaker should consider in building a more prosperous future for all Americans."

—Mary Schapiro, Former Chair of the SEC

"The United States middle class is shrinking and the stressed underclass is growing. Income inequality is worsening and fracturing our country. This vital book has gathered the best minds to seek answers—both causes and remedies. For those who care, this is urgent required reading."

—Senator Don Riegle (D–MI; 1976–1994) and former Chair of the Senate Banking Committee

"This book is a call to arms. We must refocus to ensure the American Dream is available to future generations by creating more collaborations, more public-private partnerships, and investing in our infrastructure to get the job done."

—Sandy Weill, Chairman Emeritus, Citigroup, Inc.

"To help bring America together and identify the actions needed to rekindle a vigorous middle class, Gene Ludwig convened an extraordinary bipartisan, diverse group of participants with deep knowledge drawn from academia, policy formation, government, business, and community leadership. It is a highly readable action guide to doing the always unfinished work of forming a more perfect union and should be widely read."

—Mary Houghton and Ron Grzywinski, Co-founders of ShoreBank

The
Vanishing
American
Dream

The
Vanishing
American
Dream

A Frank Look at the Economic Realities
Facing Middle- and Lower-Income Americans

A Symposium at Yale Law School, April 12, 2019

Edited by GENE LUDWIG

DISRUPTION
BOOKS

New York

Published by Disruption Books
New York, NY
www.disruptionbooks.com

Distributed by Disruption Books

For ordering information or special discounts for bulk purchases, please contact Disruption Books at info@disruptionbooks.com.

Print ISBN: 978-1-63331-044-5
eBook ISBN: 978-1-63331-045-2

Library of Congress Cataloging-in-Publication Data

Names: Ludwig, Eugene Allan, 1946- editor.
Title: The vanishing American dream : a frank look at the economic
   realities facing middle- and lower-income Americans : a symposium at
   Yale Law School, April 12, 2019 / edited by Gene Ludwig.
Description: First edition. | New York : Disruption Books, [2020] |
   Includes bibliographical references and index.
Identifiers: LCCN 2020015905 (print) | LCCN 2020015906 (ebook) | ISBN
   9781633310445 (hardback) | ISBN 9781633310452 (epub)
Subjects: LCSH: Income distribution—United States. | American Dream. |
   Middle class—United States. | Poor—United States. | United
   States—Economic conditions—21st century. | United States—Economic
   Policy—2009-
Classification: LCC HC110.I5 V36 2020 (print) | LCC HC110.I5 (ebook) |
   DDC 339.2/20973—dc23
LC record available at https://lccn.loc.gov/2020015905
LC ebook record available at https://lccn.loc.gov/2020015906

Cover and text design by Sheila Parr
Cover image ©Shutterstock / Christian Hinkle

First Edition

This book is dedicated to my wife Carol along with my children Abigail, Elizabeth, and David and my brother Ken.

Contents

Preface

The COVID-19 Storm

When, in 2018, I first approached Dean Heather Gerken about hosting a forum at Yale Law School on the plight of lower- and middle-income Americans, I was driven primarily to address a masked and increasingly grave deterioration in the nation's economic environment for that specific but enormous segment of the population. Amid a raft of seemingly very positive economic indicators—a low unemployment rate, strong GDP growth, buoyant market benchmarks—I had concluded that too few policymakers were taking heed of the fact that many communities were being left behind. Too frequently, Washington insiders seemed sanguine that wealth accruing at the top of the income scale would eventually "trickle down" to the rest of the country. A closer look at localities like the place where I grew up—York, Pennsylvania—revealed that thinking to be entirely off base. And York's experience wasn't unique. It was reflected in neglected corners of thriving cities, in hollowed-out rural communities, and thousands of other American towns and small cities as well.

A year after the Yale forum, and just before this book was scheduled to go to press, the nation was both newly laid low by the economic crisis precipitated by the COVID-19 pandemic and newly enraged by the scourge of racial inequality. Americans are losing faith in their nation's promise. The unemployment rate is 14.7 percent overall—but 21.2 percent for those without a high school degree.[1] At the forum a year before, many of us had anticipated a recession. But the downturn now appears significantly deeper even than what the nation faced amid the financial crisis of 2008. So, positive economic indicators no longer *obscure* our understanding of the economy's declining health because, well, there are very few positive economic indicators to speak of.

That's why the substance of our conversation in the spring of 2019 is more relevant, important, and resonant than ever. The wisdom shared over the course of that day, among a group amassed from the top echelons of academia, policy, business, and banking, anticipated many of today's challenges—but dangers lurk today that existed beyond the scope of our conversation in 2019. That adds a new urgency to the tenor of our conversation. As is now utterly clear, we do not live in a Panglossian world where most believe that "all is for the best in the best of all possible worlds." The protests that erupted after George Floyd's murder make clear that we've done too little even during good times to address the ongoing legacy of racism. And yet it would appear some of the same myopia that spurred policymakers to ignore the plight of lower- and middle-class Americans before the crisis is now steering efforts to shape the recovery.

That continued blindness is reflected in a view, prevalent in some circles of Washington, that bailing out the markets—even the junk bond market that largely serves the most sophisticated investors—is of more vital importance than serving those most directly affected by the downturn. This perverse thinking perhaps emerges from a presumption that this will be a fairly short-term and contained crisis, such that we do not need to put the time and effort into dealing with the longer-term disequilibrium that was so apparent before the virus infected the American economy. Excuses for not taking more transformational steps are thoroughly misguided. But much as they echo the same mistaken assumptions that led policymakers to misunderstand the economy through the course of the last recovery, these excuses are particularly noxious as the country faces what can be described as an economic tsunami.

Here's the overriding point: When a tsunami strikes a tropical island, everyone may be affected, but the storm's destructive power will not be equally distributed. Those who live in poorer circumstances, often in the low-lying ports, generally suffer the worst of the storm. A closer look at what's happening in the wake of COVID-19 reveals the same dynamic. The damage is not equally distributed. A family's ability to ride out a catastrophe is explicitly tied to their preexisting circumstances. And that prospect then speaks to the approach policymakers should take moving forward.

When the Boxing Day Tsunami ravaged coastal communities across the rim of the Indian Ocean in 2004, President George W. Bush appointed his two predecessors—Bill Clinton and George H. W. Bush—to lead international efforts to aid in the recovery. As Clinton often explained in the months and years that followed, their joint bipartisan efforts weren't designed to return these decimated communities to the places they had been before the violent waves had crashed on the shores. Instead, the aim was to help these communities "build back better"—to make them more prosperous and secure than they had been before. That meant dealing with the very problems that had left many so vulnerable in the first place.

That same principle should be applied to the American economy today. Perhaps nothing could have equipped us to thwart entirely the current pandemic—though, as many have argued, policymakers could have prepared and responded much more effectively. Either way, this should not distract us from a more important principle: Every American should have a genuine opportunity to earn a living wage through a job that provides enough income for their family to have food, health care, a good education, some savings, and a solid roof over their heads. That principle should guide our priorities. Nursing the economy back to health means not only stimulating new demand in the short term, but also clearing a new, wider, more robust path for Americans of all races, genders, backgrounds, and economic circumstances to achieve, in earnest, the American Dream.

Divergent Opportunity—A Long Trend

As policymakers think more systematically about how to breathe new life into the American Dream—to make it available to Americans in every community, irrespective of race—they need to begin by distinguishing those challenges that have been born from the crisis from those that pre-date the present misery. Which are acute, and which are chronic? In the pages that follow, some of America's leading minds predominantly discuss the latter topic. But it bears emphasizing that while many at the top of the economic heap will remember the long economic expansion book-ended by the Great Recession and the COVID-19 pandemic as a period of optimism and exuberance, the truth is that for most middle- and lower-income Americans, it was a period of increasing economic struggle.

Virtually everyone at the 2019 conference agreed that access to the American Dream had been narrowing for middle- and low-income Americans for years. That truth had simply been obscured by misleading topline-biased economic indices. In the first two decades of the twenty-first century, wage growth of the ninetieth percentile of income earners outpaced those at the twenty-fifth percentile by nearly 25 percent.[2] Maybe even more important, the costs of basic necessities—rent, education, health care—had risen much faster than incomes among those living nearer the middle to bottom of the wage scale. In other words, for many, true prosperity was slipping away even in the "good times."

But of course, the divergence wasn't evenly distributed among those accounting for each point on the income scale. The great scourge of our nation's history—racism—ran rampant as well. Over the last decade before the crisis, median wages for Black workers grew more slowly than even a decade earlier. So, much as a young Black man in a predominantly minority neighborhood in Brooklyn, for example, and a young white woman growing up in York, Pennsylvania, might both justifiably have felt frustrated by discrimination, the challenge was likely even more acute for the Black man and his family. In 2019, prior to the COVID-19 tsunami, the median white family had $171,000 worth of wealth holdings, compared with the median Black family's meager $17,150.[3]

The impact of the chronic, tectonic downward shift for middle- and lower-income Americans was reflected not only in the income and wealth data, but in the way Americans had been handling their finances. Delinquency skyrocketed during the 2008 recession on a range of loans—on mortgage debt most notably, but also on credit card, home equity, and auto debt. Those numbers fell quickly as the economy recovered. But student loan delinquency kept growing and then plateaued through the subsequent recovery. After falling, credit card debt began to grow again as well. Coming into the COVID-19 crisis, consumer debt was at an all-time high, while wealth and liquidity were low—creating a witches' brew for even more pain among low- and moderate-income families. And that's where America was when the virus began to wreak havoc.

The American Dream Even Further from Reach

Much is being lost in our focus on the immediate and acute crisis: In fact, the wreckage is tied explicitly to the longer-term and chronic problems endemic to the underlying economy. At the 2019 conference, attendees placed a heavy emphasis on access to education. As several participants noted, in the places where people felt most deeply the sense that they were barely managing to stay afloat, college degrees were few and far between. So then, which jobs has the pandemic eliminated? Those available to individuals who have not yet graduated with a bachelor's degree. Mere weeks into the pandemic, all the job gains low- and medium-skill workers had made over the previous decade of recovery had vanished.[4]

Furthermore, it's not just whether people still have their jobs; even those who can still claim an employer are working fewer hours. And whose jobs have been curtailed the most? Not long into the crisis, non-college-educated workers had seen their work time decline on average by 6.6 hours per week, a trend most pronounced in goods-producing industries.[5] By contrast, those with a college degree had seen their hours decrease by a mere 3.4 hours. Less than a third of upper-income households reported a job loss or a pay cut—but in lower-income households, that figure was slightly more than half.[6]

The racial split reflects the same divergence, with the pandemic serving as a shock by exacerbating previous trends. More than three in five Hispanic Americans reported in April 2020 that someone in their household had lost a job or was taking a pay cut. The same was true of more than two in five Black Americans. Both of these figures outstripped the percentage of whites in the same situation.[7] And young people, whose prospects have dimmed through the decades, are bearing a disproportionate percent of the burden here as well: More than seven in ten workers younger than age thirty reported working fewer hours, compared with 55 percent of those between ages forty and fifty-five.[8]

Pointing out that these effects reflect, in no small measure, the broader historical context does nothing to belittle the depth of the present economic crisis. If the American Dream was slipping away for a vast portion of the population before the virus came to the United States, it has unquestionably fallen farther out of reach since the beginning of 2020. And that speaks to the central question facing policymakers, the private sector, and nonprofit leaders looking to steer the nation back on track: What, exactly, are we supposed to do now?

Never Waste a Crisis

In the face of the pandemic's sudden impact, government was absolutely right to enact immediate countermeasures, even if the particulars deserve additional scrutiny down the line. Wisely, state and local leaders—sometimes with the federal government's help—stepped in to mitigate the spread, equip the nation's public health facilities to care for those infected by the virus, and stimulate new demand. But in May 2020, as I write this note, policymakers are slowly beginning to shift to a longer-term focus. This years-long effort, like those that followed the 2004 tsunami, needs to be designed to help Americans "build back better."

Here's what's so remarkable: The long-term strategy best equipped to preserve the American Dream is, almost without exception, the same today as when this august gathering of luminaries met to discuss the topic in the spring of 2019. America's enduring resiliency depends most squarely on the element that has long made America "exceptional." Namely, we need to build an economy that gives everyone, including those in more marginalized communities—urban, suburban, and rural alike—an opportunity to give their children a better life than they had growing up.

As the scholars, practitioners, and business leaders who assembled in New Haven made clear, there is no one "secret sauce" to rebuilding the economic ladder that once allowed those without means to climb up over the course of a lifetime of hard work. But we can make a series of investments and choices that will, in the end, make a world of difference. We could, at long last, make our educational system an extraordinary system for everyone, in particular by adapting it to the demands of the twenty-first-century economy. At the height of the unemployment stemming from the 2008 crisis, many employers could not find people properly trained to fill their open positions. That will be the case even more this time if we don't take action. The jobs of tomorrow require better training today, and policymakers need to take dramatic action to ensure access to that education.

Similarly, at this moment when global interest rates are remarkably and historically low, America must invest in twenty-first-century infrastructure in ways that benefit not only the very rich but those much further down the economic pecking order, indeed all the way to the bottom. In the aftermath of the crisis, Washington will need to invest much more in the research facilities required to keep the population productive and safe (including from another public health emergency) in our increasingly globalized and technologically sophisticated world. But even beyond that, our roads, bridges, ports, rails, broadband, and more are in serious need of updating. And we should improve America's trade balance by leading the world into a green-energy economy instead of being dragged behind it.

There are too many good ideas in the pages that follow for me to include an exhaustive list—but the point remains: The key to the nation's long-term success and the rehabilitation of the American Dream is much the same today as it was in 2019. If we do not grasp the moment and redress what has become a seriously negative, secular trend, further decline and social unrest will become inevitable.

I remain gratified that so many experts came together to discuss such a crucial topic. This record of that discussion remains available to infuse ongoing debates about public policy with real wisdom. And most fundamentally, I'm optimistic that the United States, which has overcome such vast challenges in the past, will rebound again to provide broad-based opportunity, prosperity, and security to Americans of every creed, background, and station.

—E.A.L.

Notes

1   "Unemployment rates for persons 25 years and older by educational attainment," Graphics for Economic News Releases, U.S. Bureau of Labor Statistics, https://www.bls.gov/charts/employment-situation/unemployment-rates-for-persons-25-years-and-older-by-educational-attainment.htm.

2   "Weekly and hourly earnings data from the Current Population Survey," U.S. Bureau of Labor Statistics, https://data.bls.gov/PDQWeb/le.

3   "Median Value of Family Net Worth," Tax Policy Center, March 11, 2019, https://www.taxpolicycenter.org/fiscal-fact/median-value-wealth-race-ff03112019.

4   Current Employment Statistics Survey, U.S. Bureau of Labor Statistics, April 2020, https://beta.bls.gov.

5   "Average weekly hours of production employees," Graphics for Economic News Releases, U.S. Bureau of Labor Statistics, April 2020, https://www.bls.gov/charts/employment-situation/average-weekly-hours-of-production-employees.htm.

6   Kim Parker, Juliana Menasce Horowitz, and Anna Brown, "About Half of Lower-Income Americans Report Household Job or Wage Loss Due to COVID-19," Pew Research Center, April 21, 2020, https://www.pewsocialtrends.org/2020/04/21/about-half-of-lower-income-americans-report-household-job-or-wage-loss-due-to-covid-19/.

7   Ibid.

8   Abi Adams-Prassl, Teodora Boneva, Marta Golin, and Christopher Rauh, "Inequality in the Impact of the Coronavirus Shock: New Survey Evidence in the US," April 1, 2020, https://drive.google.com/file/d/16sp-8tm7t1kmFM-zL6bxTNlKHcCupNLP/view.

Introduction

Seeing the American Economy Through a Glass, Darkly

I am, without question, the beneficiary of privilege. I'm white and male. I'm an English-speaking American citizen. I've been blessed both to receive a terrific public education and to find wonderful mentors throughout my career. And as much as I've certainly worked hard to make the most of my opportunities, I'm also acutely aware that my privilege was born primarily of luck.

That luck began at birth. My parents provided me a childhood that might well have been taken straight from a Norman Rockwell painting. Mom and Dad, both of whom had lived through the Great Depression and World War II, were living, breathing testaments to the American Dream. They exemplified the notion that hard work, tenacity, and determination could help nearly any family provide their children more opportunity than the previous generation enjoyed.[1]

But it wasn't just my parents who made me lucky. It was the place I was raised. Few could have been luckier than to be raised, like me, in the vibrant and dynamic region surrounding York, Pennsylvania.

Canaries in an Economic Coal Mine

You don't hear much about York these days. Frankly, residents of the more "cosmopolitan" regions of the country—places that are so solidly blue, you might not find a Trump voter within ten blocks of any given artisanal coffee shop—probably haven't heard of it.

A generation ago, political commentator James Carville slandered the region where I grew up, quipping that the Keystone State is nothing but "Pittsburgh and Philadelphia with Alabama in between"[2] (or something to that effect). But that's not what I recall growing up in South Central Pennsylvania. In the 1940s, '50s, and '60s, York represented the best of the American economy, promising a shot at the American Dream to anyone willing to give it their all.

I don't mean to suggest there were no problems. Bigotry against Black Americans, in particular, was sometimes fierce. York is situated not too far north of the Mason-Dixon Line, and there were significant parts of town where Black Americans, Catholics, and Jews—my family included—knew not to live. But even amidst the prejudice, the middle-class ethos that suffused nearly every aspect of life pulled people who might otherwise have faced dire circumstances into more comfortable, prosperous rhythms of life. York was an opportunity factory.

The region was geographically diverse. Rural areas boasted beautiful orchards; farmers tilled fields and harvested spring and summer fruits and vegetables. At the same time, York boasted a strong industrial economy. York Dental Supply, York Air Conditioner, York Barbell, Harley-Davidson, Edgcomb Steel, Caterpillar Tractor, and AMP all had either headquarters or bustling facilities in York County. And these companies were deeply intertwined with the local community. Town lore suggests that even during the depths of the Great Depression, York hummed to the point that the community did not lose a single bank. It had a remarkable and nearly unblemished reputation. Almost without interruption, York was prosperous from the 1700s through 1970.

But then things changed.

Today, York and an untoward number of struggling industrial American communities like it around the country—places like Flint, Michigan, and Albany, Georgia—have been forgotten by cosmopolitan America. Where they were once springboards to the American Dream, with people like me lucky to have been raised there, today they are at best economic backwaters, acting almost like economic quicksand preventing present-day residents from climbing the ladder toward prosperity.

Quite frankly, York—with Baltimore's suburbs and Washington, D.C., within striking distance—is better positioned than many other communities facing similar challenges. But to visit today, which I have had occasion to do, you can't help but conclude that the area is in rough shape. "Flyover country," once the backbone of the American economy, has not only fallen behind. It has become, in too many cases, a drag on the nation's prosperity.

It's not just York, of course. And it's not just the places that pundits have chosen to study since President Donald Trump's unexpected victory in 2016. Even in pockets of the most prosperous cities in America, working- and middle-class families are struggling to keep their heads above water.

You need not travel all the way to York to see the evidence. Simply have a look at the tent city situated just outside the Federal Reserve in Washington . . . or see the homeless sleeping beside the gleaming skyscrapers in San Francisco . . . or take a subway to the more forlorn neighborhoods of New York City's outer boroughs. Housing prices are beyond reach. Getting to work means making an impossibly long commute. Wages are low at the jobs many can access, forcing them to live in places where crime is rampant, schools are chaotic, the water is poisoned, and decay is the norm.

The pain has not been spread evenly. Black Americans, marginalized for hundreds of years, are still burdened by challenges that dramatically narrow their economic base and deplete their opportunities to live the American Dream. And that's as true in East New York and on the South Side of Chicago as it is in Flint, Michigan, and Albany, Georgia.

But as indelible a role as race plays in the disparity, it's only one part of the story. The challenge isn't just urban, and it isn't just rural. Poverty is rising in the nation's suburbs as well. Those struggling to keep their heads above water may be living blocks from places that are awash in prosperity, or hundreds of miles away, or somewhere in between. But the reality is, that chasm between the people thriving in today's economy and those unable to get ahead has been widening for far too long.

What's so remarkable, even as the evidence mounts that portions of the population are living in destitution or on the precipice of destitution, is that the prevailing economic analysis of 2019 says that the economy is humming. It's almost as though we're living in a fantasyland. And what's most worrisome about all the happy talk is that it may spur policymakers to ignore indicators that would otherwise serve as canaries in the coal mine.

This isn't just a question of equal opportunity—though that's a crucial aspect. The economic plight of working- and middle-class families is bound to have a broader economic impact, destabilizing the economic growth wealthier neighborhoods continue to enjoy. If whole communities of Americans are left to raise their children amid scarcity, their plight is poised to eclipse the prosperity that exists in the tonier parts of America. And that will almost certainly tip off a vicious cycle.

This story can be told through research and data. But for me, the narrative is clearest when I can see and touch the phenomenon in all its horror. And there's no escaping it in York.

Each time I return home, I'm taken aback. Poverty is now endemic in portions of York County that were once solidly middle or working class. Within the Hanover Area School District, a corner of the community where most students were once the children of self-sufficient farmers and industrious factory workers, nearly two-thirds of students are eligible for free or reduced-price lunches.[3] The heroin and opioid epidemics have hit York hard, with more residents dying of drug overdoses than of car crashes.[4] After a 90 percent increase year-over-year in heroin-related deaths, the county coroner labeled 2017 the "worst year ever."[5]

It's easy enough to offer prosaic explanations for the pervasive rough sledding: Factories closed. Globalization pushed corporations to send the jobs overseas. Racism abounds. But for those who really want to understand what's going on, those more superficial answers only prompt more thoughtful questions.

What changed to make it so that York and communities like it, many of which managed to thrive during previous economic transitions, were unable to adapt this time? Why hasn't Washington been more responsive to the needs of communities like York—and what could the government do to turn things around? What responsibility does the private sector have—and what might business leaders do if they decided that York's economic survival was important to their long-term growth strategy?

On a trip back to York the year after Trump's victory, I became convinced that Washington still hadn't figured things out. Sure, national publications had commissioned a long litany of articles detailing the economic anxieties in the heartland, with reporters traipsing into diners and asking patrons whether they were concerned that a local plant might shut down.[6] Other important reporting exposed how racism has been woven into the very fabric of American culture—a reality too frequently overlooked.

But York's current suffering, like that in various communities around the country, hasn't grown simply out of the fact that a few plants moved out, or because racism has become more pointed. Something even more dramatic is going on. And if the more superficial explanations weren't painting a complete picture, I thought policymakers and the general public alike would benefit from a more in-depth examination.

In that spirit, in April 2019, I helped organize a bipartisan symposium to study the plight of America's low- and moderate-income segments. Having graduated from Yale Law School, I sought out the current dean, Heather Gerken, and she generously offered to let me host the event on campus. Dean Gerken immediately understood why the effort was worthy of the law school's participation. As she explained in her opening remarks, "Lawyers grapple with inequality's consequences every single day, but they tend to deploy a fairly narrow range of tools in their efforts. [At Yale Law School], we encourage our students to look beyond the existing tools. Today, we have a chance to interrogate long-held orthodoxies regarding markets, fiscal and monetary policy—even the relationship between elite institutions that all of us represent and an economic system that is not working for many."

We invited some of the most sophisticated minds from across the political spectrum to gather in a closed setting, and we were blown away by the eagerness of these august figures—a former state governor, a former Treasury secretary from a Democratic administration, a former chair of the Council of Economic Advisers in a Republican administration, a former deputy Treasury secretary and Federal Reserve governor, a former president of the Chicago Fed, a mayor, a Nobel Prize–winning economist, two CEOs, and a range of academics—to address what so many think is among the most important challenges of our time. I wanted to frame the agenda in a way that would prompt a frank discussion about what's gone wrong; why the problems aren't being solved; and what might be done, on both the national and local levels, to turn things around for poor Americans and for the working and middle classes.

This volume memorializes the day's conversation and debate, collecting in one place the wisdom offered by some of the nation's leading minds on a vexing topic. More than that, it offers policymakers and historians a window into what I believe is the most serious and underappreciated economic challenge facing the United States ahead of the 2020 presidential election. Left unaddressed, I fear, the challenges we discussed at the conference could undermine both America's system of free enterprise and our democratic institutions. As the following dialogue reveals, however, our nation's leaders—in both the public and private spheres—have a number of tools they could use to address the growing plight.

This introduction is an account of what I personally took away from the conference. Because the group included experts with a range of perspectives and experiences, the discussion was frequently lively, if not raucous—and it was constructive, if not contentious. No two participants saw eye to eye on every issue, but fortunately there was broad agreement on some of the overarching themes. My hope is that the ideas pondered during the course of the discussion, now memorialized here, will provide both perspective on how we arrived here and guidance for those working to drive broader-based prosperity in years and decades to come.

The Truth Behind the Prevailing Analysis

Conversations about the American economy tend to fall into one of two authentic but incomplete narratives. The first, more frequently touted by Republicans now that a Republican occupies the White House, is that the American economy is incredibly strong. (Of course, Democrats embraced largely the same narrative when a Democrat was sitting in the Oval Office.) By certain measures, there simply isn't any denying the veracity of that contention. In the summer of 2019, even as trade tensions were ratcheting up with China, America was enjoying the fruits of the longest peacetime economic expansion in the nation's history.[7] The S&P 500 had repeatedly hit new record highs.[8] Traditional measures of national unemployment had fallen to shocking lows.[9]

The second conversation, more frequently heard from the left, points out—also quite accurately—that America is becoming increasingly unequal. In ways unseen since the Gilded Age, the spoils of prosperity accrue today disproportionately to the richest of the rich. As longtime business executive Andrew Tisch pointed out at the conference, the ratio of a CEO's pay to the average worker's pay has grown exponentially, from 30-to-1 in 1978 to 270-to-1 today.[10] Amid all the ripple effects of that shift, wealth has skewed successively over time, with the rich getting richer and everyone else falling behind.

Some of that has to do with our educational system. As Yale Law School professor Daniel Markovits affirmed, elite graduate programs now funnel high-performing students (many with families capable of paying for their degrees) into professional opportunities that are lucrative in ways that are entirely beyond the reach of most other American families:

> *Whereas there was basically no professional school premium or gradu-ate school premium to wages in 1970, today, someone without a high school degree has only about a 1-in-75 chance of earning as much over her lifetime as the median professional school graduate. Some-body with only a high school degree—that's roughly two-thirds of the population—has only a 1-in-40 chance of earning as much. Someone with only a BA has only about a 1-in-6 chance of earning as much as the median professional school graduate.*[11]

That thesis was burnished by Yale political scientist Jacob Hacker. "We have seen not only rising inequality across individuals but rising inequality across regions,"[12] he explained. "The U.S. is distinctive in seeing a sharp rise at the top that is coupled with a sharp decline for the bottom half of the population. . . . It used to be that cities seemed to have this kind of positive [employment] spillover, so that the lower-wage workforce was doing a lot better in the cities." He asserted that for people of lower income today, there's essentially a flat line—"basically no relationship between population density and wages."

These changes are crucial to any complete understanding of what's happening inside America's economy. But while the aggregate and comparative views of the US economy shed important beams of light, a broader reality too frequently goes unremarked. Whatever the broad-based economic indicators may suggest, and however you measure the widening chasm between the very rich and everyone else, the most important indicator is how low- and moderate-income families view their own prospects. How do their prospects change from one generation to the next? Are people being offered opportunities to succeed as their par-ents or grandparents did?

By that measure, many in America are truly in a crisis. Throughout the country, in pockets of prosperous urban areas, in suburban communities often ignored in national economic narratives, and particularly in places such as York, Flint, and Albany, life has gotten more difficult compared with life in the previous several decades. The economy has become less rewarding, and the American Dream is slipping away. Without denying the underlying truth of any other single analysis, that reality deserves serious attention entirely on its own.

Brookings scholar Isabel Sawhill arrived at the conference having recently published a book that surveys the reality on the ground in much of America. In her research, she traveled around the country asking people what class they considered themselves. Were they middle class? Working class?

One woman replied, "I'm in the hanging-on-by-your-fingernails class."

Why? As Sawhill explained, "Wages, especially for the less educated or less skilled, have been flat or declining,[13] [while] employment rates have declined, especially amongst men.[14] . . . And instead of being in the top ranks in terms of labor force participation, compared to other advanced countries, we are now falling way down in the ranking on how many people are working."[15] Understandably, she acknowledged, that has left many Americans feeling "very insecure . . . very replaceable."

Andrea Levere, the former president of Prosperity Now, argued that the real issue driving income volatility (as opposed to inequality) is financial instability. Prosperity Now's research revealed that "13.2 percent of households fell behind on their bills, and those with volatile incomes did so twice as much."[16] And that reality was particularly concentrated in certain communities: 63 percent of Black households and Latino households, she explained, are living in liquid-asset poverty.[17] All of this is to say that the standard narratives about America's economy—that it's going strong, and that the rich are getting richer—obscure another objective truth: Middle- and lower-income families have fared worse over the decades.[18] And particularly when compared with how the economy looks on paper, they are in a deeper hole than in previous generations.[19]

Conference attendees did not agree on everything. But almost everyone in the room appeared to share the view that whatever economic policies have been emerging from government, and whatever approach companies are taking to maximize their returns, the underlying reality is an unacceptable outcome for a vast portion of the population. If these trends continue, the suffering will not be contained to those currently affected—it will inevitably grow to encompass more of the American population and spread even to healthier portions of the economy. If policymakers and executives do not begin solving for this challenge before the next economic downturn, we may soon reach a point where it's too late. So we need to begin making adjustments now.

Demystifying the Broader Economic Landscape: What Has Changed?

By some measure, the pundits and analysts who have obscured the plight of working- and middle-class America should be given a pass. After all, the indicators we use to gauge whether things are headed in the right direction measure only a sliver of what really matters. In a world of increasing data sophistication, the broadly accepted standards of measurement—national GDP, job aggregates, and unemployment figures—whistle past what is happening in places like York, Flint, and Albany, let alone other discrete areas of economic deprivation. Yet those are the conventional ways we gauge the economy's health from month to month and from year to year.

It seems like a simple point, but you can't overstate how the prism through which we view the economy affects the choices businesses and policymakers make about how to shape the future. When the Federal Reserve or the Bureau of Labor Statistics publishes economic data each month, policymakers invariably make judgments that can nudge a certain sector of the economy in a healthy direction while decimating everyone else. Several conference participants made this very point. Our continued dependence on aggregate US economic data is clouding our understanding of what's happening on the ground. We need to focus on new measures if we're going to understand what's really going on.

As former deputy Treasury secretary and Federal Reserve board governor Sarah Bloom Raskin argued, gross domestic product may be the gold standard today for measuring a society's overall economic well-being, but it presents a particularly distorted picture. As a senior editor of *The Financial Times* wrote once, "It is the sum total of everything we produce over a given period. It includes cars built, Beethoven symphonies played, and broadband connections made. But it also counts plastic waste bobbing in the ocean, burglar alarms and petrol consumed while stuck in traffic." [20]

Moreover, GDP is a terrible measure of productivity—it actually declines if a company figures out how to produce the same product at a lower cost. [21] Maybe of even greater concern, as Raskin argued, it does not measure unpaid work like childcare or eldercare, meaning that crucial sectors of the economy aren't represented whatsoever in the most important figure we use to gauge the economy's overall health. [22]

Perhaps even more distorting is our traditional measure of unemployment. Most thoughtful analysts are keenly aware that unemployment figures are misleading. To start with, frustrated job seekers who have given up on the possibility of landing a new position no longer count among the "unemployed"; their decision to drop out of the workforce actually improves the rate. But it's worse than that.

Unemployment figures do not adjust for salary figures, employment benefits, health care coverage, or pensions. So when people in comfortable middle-class jobs are laid off and accept more marginal positions that barely lift them out of poverty, the unemployment figures do not budge. [23] [24] Levere noted that members of the Federal Reserve's Community Advisory Council, which she chaired, have convinced Fed economists that "the two data points [of] unemployment and inflation rates do not describe what is really happening in their communities." [25] [26]

It's not just that big aggregates like GDP and unemployment brush over important distinctions within the economy; they also fail to account for the sorts of changes that people feel in their own communities. Nor do they shed any light on important economic factors such as whether certain portions of the population can get a loan to grow a business or access a mortgage to purchase a home. Mary Miller, a former under secretary of the Treasury Department, explained, "We pulled all of that data on the banks in Baltimore, and it is really shocking how old it is, how irrelevant it is—how it doesn't measure small business lending."[27]

This is not to say that there's no value in GDP, unemployment, or other aggregate figures. But at a time when we know inequality is worsening, policymakers shouldn't weight these figures so heavily when making decisions. They need ready access to a much wider range of more granular data—figures measuring income, wealth, liquidity, debt, and other related data. Moreover, those measures need to be broken down by geographic area, by ethnicity, by gender, by age, by level of income, and by job category.

Without that sort of granular data, policymakers and even PhD economists frequently find it too difficult to understand what's actually happening on the ground. As a result, Washington makes decisions designed simply to improve the aggregates. And as we've seen, decisions made in that context tend to leave people living in places like York, Flint, and Albany—not to mention other forlorn communities—far behind.

Few (if any) of the conference participants dissented during discussions of the underlying problem—namely, the increasing level of misery and despair felt by people in various pockets of America. And the group generally agreed that traditional measures of economic prosperity distort the underlying reality. But when the discussion turned to the question of *why* communities are being left behind—why, for example, was York able to thrive for 250 years, only to be upended over the past half century?—consensus in the room began to scatter. Nevertheless, the group eventually coalesced broadly (and with exceptions) around a general sense of what's wrong.

Washington Post business and economics columnist Steven Pearlstein offered an explanation that many on the center left, including me, find both convincing and concerning:

> *Because of globalization, technology, deregulation, and changes in business norms, the benefits of economic growth have largely been captured by people at the top. The result has been—for most people, I think—an unacceptable increase in inequality of income and wealth and therefore opportunity, which has polarized our politics and rendered our government dysfunctional to the point that it now threatens our prosperity and our democracy.*

He continued, "Technology has caused some people to become very wealthy and have high incomes, and other people, low incomes. So the people who created the word processor are richer, and the people who used to type on typewriters are poorer."[28]

Many of the people attending the conference probably expected Pearlstein's comments to be accepted without objection. But Oren Cass, a senior fellow at the conservative Manhattan Institute, countered with an alternative thesis—one that also has a great deal to speak for it. Far from focusing on macroeconomics and innovation, Cass focused on wages. "Labor market outcomes have taken an extraordinary turn for the worse over the past thirty or forty years," he revealed.

> *Particularly for men—particularly for those without college degrees. The most striking way to see this is just to look at median earnings for a man with a high school degree and compare it to the poverty line.[29] In 1975, a typical man with a high school degree could support a family of four at more than twice the poverty line. The comparable man today can only clear the poverty line by less than 40 percent.*

Things are especially bad for young people, Cass concluded:

> *If you look at 25-to-34-year-olds, for instance, the share earning less*
> *than $30,000 a year has gone up from a quarter in the '70s to more*
> *than 40 percent now. That is including folks with college degrees.*
> *If you were to look specifically at those without college degrees, the*
> *picture would be even more dire.*[30] *It seems to me that the central*
> *problem we're having, and the one that then feeds into a lot of the sta-*
> *tistics . . . is that people can't actually find jobs that are going to allow*
> *them to support their families, to build careers and wealth over time.*

Cass's observation points to a profound reality: Solid work with solid remuneration isn't just a means to a more prosperous existence—it's good in and of itself. Honest work is ennobling, whatever the nature of that underlying contribution may be. It imparts a set of values and character-building strengths that contribute to a worker's sense of worth and thus to society as a whole. Yes, America should be ashamed that people who mean to play by the rules can't earn enough to support a middle-class lifestyle. But we should worry just as much about the downstream effects when people can't find opportunities to apply their own hard work and self-discipline to the challenge of growing the American economy.

Regardless of whether you find Pearlstein's or Cass's view more convincing—I think there's a great deal of truth in both lines of reasoning—the end result is the same. And so the question quickly becomes: What do you do about it? How do you buttress the middle and working classes against the pressures that come with digitization and globalization? What can you do to create opportunities—in urban, suburban, and rural places alike—for families to earn a middle-class wage?

That discussion turns back to a fundamental economic principle: supply and demand. All too often, the focus on GDP, unemployment, and inequality obscures the gap that has opened between what sorts of labor the economy needs and what sorts working- and middle-class Americans are equipped to provide. And that's where the conference participants next focused their attention.

An Epic Mismatch

It would be one thing if technological and geopolitical changes (read: globalization) had sapped demand for the sorts of work that people without a fancy education could perform. The "guaranteed minimum income" proposal that's celebrated today in some circles presumes that large swaths of the American population no longer have useful professional roles to play—that as technology (machine learning, artificial intelligence, and so forth) becomes more sophisticated, whole classes of humanity will be rendered economically useless, such that they will need to be supported by massive wealth redistribution.

But at the conference, several participants explicitly rejected this dystopian fear. There's no doubt that many Americans feel as though they're being left behind. The research that Belle Sawhill and Oren Cass have done, interviewing people in Syracuse, New York; Greensboro, North Carolina; and St. Louis, Missouri, found both that wages were more meager (compared with costs, if not outright) and that adults were often overwhelmed by feelings of despair.[31] But what's so remarkable—and possibly hope-inducing—is that employers are actually desperate to hire a new legion of workers, presuming that those new hires can be trained to perform certain tasks.

The statistics are remarkable—if, for some, unexpected. One 2019 survey found a big uptick in the share of businesses reporting that "finding talent" was their foremost problem. Nearly nine out of ten businesses looking to hire reported that they couldn't find qualified applicants.[32] Why does the American economy suffer from such an epic mismatch?

A range of possible explanations exist. But one crucial factor centers on how employees are supposed to glean new skills. As employers have scaled back their investments in training—a trend born, in part, from fear that newly trained workers sometimes jump to a job at a competing firm—a beleaguered population of workers no longer has sufficient opportunities to pick up the skills in demand by would-be employers. The results are not unexpected: One report from the Bureau of Labor Statistics found that there were far more job openings in June 2019 than there were hires.[33]

Former Massachusetts governor Deval Patrick delivered the conference's keynote address and focused on this very issue—the fact that the American economy isn't producing a workforce capable of filling today's demand for what he calls "middle skills" labor:

> *What the employers were telling us was, they just couldn't find the people they needed for the jobs they had, or the skills for the jobs they had[34]—many of those so-called middle skills. There's got to be a better word, but that's a term, and I think you know what I mean: more than a high school diploma but not necessarily a college degree.*

Indeed, as former Federal Reserve Bank of Chicago president Michael Moskow pointed out at the conference, for as much as contemporary analysis suggests that anyone with a computer and an internet connection can tap into the global economy, place—and specifically the talent congregated in any given place—is often determinative of where firms decide to locate their offices. "With all the problems we have with financial instability and the publicity on the violence [in Chicago]," he maintained, "the most important single factor in attracting firms to Chicago is the quality of the workforce. That's number one by far. The firms that are looking to locate will [ask], 'Do you have a quality workforce?'"

So here's the central rub in America's economy today: Businesses aren't flocking to places like York, Flint, and Albany, in large part because the local population doesn't boast the set of skills that those businesses need to grow. And in too many cases, when businesses do locate there, and when people move in from outside the community to fill those jobs, the effect is simply to displace local residents who have no entrée to the new jobs on offer—and to raise costs for families that may have lived in certain neighborhoods for generations. And that reality really points to two possible challenges.

First, the people living in beleaguered communities need the "middle skills" to thrive—and the truth is, as several conference participants testified, our education system simply is not equipped today to provide that sort of education. I received a terrific education at the public high school I attended in York two generations ago. But when I arrived at college, I watched a whole class of bright students who'd graduated from lousy high schools flunk out through no fault of their own—they hadn't been equipped ahead of time to succeed. That's what's happening today, but perhaps on an even grander scale. I fear, but of course do not know, that the high school I attended now provides a similarly inferior education. Certainly, even if York Suburban High School remains a beacon of quality public education, too many American public schools do not.

The seemingly obvious follow-up question, then, is this: Why don't more people living in places like York, Flint, and Albany (or for that matter, in forlorn portions of America's so-called creative capitals) migrate to the places that are flush with opportunity? The short answer is that many people do. Talent is being sucked out of America's heartland at a remarkable pace, leaving the remaining population even more bereft and even further from the dream of an economic renaissance. As a recent report from the staff of Congress' Joint Economic Committee explained:

> We find that brain drain (and brain gain) states tend to fall along regional lines, although there are a number of exceptions to this general rule. Overall, dynamic states along the Boston–Washington corridor (Massachusetts, New York, New Jersey, and Maryland), on the West Coast (California, Oregon, Washington), and in other parts of the country (Illinois, Texas, Colorado, Arizona, and Hawaii) are the best at retaining and attracting highly educated adults. Meanwhile,

states in northern New England (New Hampshire and Vermont),
the Rust Belt (Pennsylvania, Ohio, Indiana, Michigan, Wisconsin,
and Missouri), the Plains (North and South Dakota and Iowa), and
the Southeast (West Virginia, Kentucky, Tennessee, South Carolina,
Alabama, Mississippi, and Louisiana), as well as Delaware, fare the
worst on both counts.[35]

It's no wonder that "free college" often polls poorly. Residents of
places that offer few opportunities to college graduates know that, with a
college degree, their children and grandchildren are almost sure to leave.[36]

Why don't others migrate? That points to the second challenge. People living in places like York, Flint, and Albany may not want to leave
their families behind in search of opportunity elsewhere in the country.
Or they may be frightened of being unable to hack it. But something
else is at work as well: They may be unable to afford the jump. As Andrea
Levere pointed out, "We developed, with an economist, the metric of
liquid-asset poverty, which determines whether [a] household has enough
savings to exist at the poverty level for just three months if their main
source of income is disrupted—such as if someone gets sick or someone
loses a job. Forty percent of US households are liquid-asset poor."[37]

It's not just that so many residents of places like York, Flint, and
Albany are poor. Worsening their plight is the fact that the places that are
thriving are so expensive. If you're struggling to keep food on the table
while paying rent in York, how are you possibly going to afford a comfortable place to live in New York or Silicon Valley? And it's not just in the
wealthy cosmopolitan communities. Where can someone working full-time at minimum wage afford a two-bedroom apartment? The research is
in, and the answer is clear: Nowhere in America is that possible.[38]

Worse, many of the places flush with opportunity are artificially expensive because existing residents use zoning and preservation laws to preclude
the construction of new housing to keep up with demand, which drives a
vicious cycle of rising rents. "It is really important to let housing supply

expand with jobs, because there are a lot of people in communities across this country where employment rates are really low, who would like to move somewhere where there are more jobs, but they're really locked out," The Hamilton Project director Jay Shambaugh explained. "Trying to make sure there are places they can live where there are jobs is really important."[39]

But of course, it's not just housing. The cost of living may be growing more rapidly in the places that are riding the wave of technological change, but it's also rising in places that are being pulled under. As Andrew Tisch noted, "The basic costs of living have spiraled upward, while family health insurance premiums and housing costs are growing twice as fast as workers' earnings.[40] And the cost of attending a four-year public school has tripled in the past thirty years."[41]

Moreover, the ability to cover the rent is really just a composite function of how much you're making and how much you pay for other goods and services—and for a whole host of reasons, costs for those goods and services have gone up. As Yale Law School professor Anika Singh Lemar, who runs the Ludwig Center for Community & Economic Development—a clinic I founded to assist low-income residents of New Haven—explained, "Housing, of course, is shorthand for a lot of different issues. It's shorthand for income problems; if your income is low, you need to lower your costs and have more affordable housing. It's shorthand for safety, trauma, school quality, the ability to accrue wealth."[42] And to cover the rising costs of those goods and services, Americans are borrowing against future income, creating a bubble that could be even more devastating than the mortgage bubble preceding the Great Recession.[43]

The Path Forward and Up

This is where conference discussions got a bit stickier. If attendees were largely on the same page about the *nature* of the challenge, and quibbled only on the margins about the root cause, there was considerably more disagreement about the choices policymakers should make in any effort to address the underlying challenges. Even when they did agree, attendees were focused on disparate ideas emanating from separate spheres.

That may not, in actuality, inhibit progress. The sheer variety of ideas suggests that Washington and our state and local leaders have a whole panoply of approaches they could employ when trying to help Americans who have been left behind. To my mind, however, certain tools should be used before others, if only because they hold more promise of having widespread impact. So what follows is largely my curated recollection of some of the ideas that really struck home. No doubt every attendee has his or her own favored policy agenda. This is mine.

Invest in America's Infrastructure

The first thing Washington ought to do is make a massive investment in America's depleted infrastructure. In economic circles, it has become almost cliché to compare America's railways and airports with those on display in Europe and Asia—particularly China. New York's LaGuardia Airport, now finally being refurbished, is a crucial gateway to the world's financial capital yet has maintained a well-deserved reputation for being among the world's most depressing air terminals. It's certainly nothing like the gleaming new facilities you see when you land in Shanghai, Hong Kong, or Singapore.

Governor Patrick made exactly this point during his keynote address when explaining why his tenure in Massachusetts was a success for such a broad-based slice of the Bay State's population:

> We invested in infrastructure, which I always describe as the unglam-orous work of government, but it supports everything else. That was about roads, rails, bridges, and airports in Boston and in Worcester, and regional airports as well, but also university buildings and labo-ratories, broadband expansion, public and affordable housing. Even health care is infrastructure—anything that creates jobs today, but also a platform for personal ambition and private investment.[44]

Former Treasury secretary Lawrence Summers made a similar point, arguing that a national infrastructure initiative would benefit the whole country. However, circumstances prompted him to add some nuance:

> *If we hadn't had the Trump tax cut, and if we didn't have quite the budget projection we have, I would have been for the trillion-dollar infrastructure, debt financed. Starting where we are now, I would probably be for the trillion-dollar infrastructure partially debt financed and partially some kind of green finance, with the ability next time the recession comes to take the financing off and have it converted into pure fiscal stimulus. If the only way I could get the infrastructure was to debt finance it, I would probably be relatively tolerant of that.*

It's not just that a revitalized infrastructure would create jobs in the course of its construction. New systems could, in many instances, connect economically deprived communities to job meccas—even when they're just across town. Mayor Luke Bronin of Hartford, Connecticut, a city that suffers from many of the challenges common among postindustrial northeastern cities, made exactly that point, saying, "One of the major constraints to accessing employment is the lack of access to . . . a meaningful public transportation network. A transportation investment could accomplish a lot of what we're talking about." Moreover, just imagine what a high-speed rail line into New York City would do for residents of the depressed but beautiful areas of the Catskills, New Haven, and greater Hartford.

At the same time, Zachary Liscow, a professor at Yale Law School, persuasively pointed out that because of the formulas Washington has devised to distribute money, even a glut of new spending on infrastructure would not necessarily help the poor. "When the Department of Transportation allocates money to projects, it does cost-benefit analyses to find the most valuable projects," he explained. "The key component in that analysis is the value of time saved in transit. The current practice by the Department of Transportation is to value the time of the poor less than the time of the rich." Liscow continued:

> *As a result, if the Department of Transportation is comparing a project—say, a bus line to help lower-income people—it will value the time of people less and be less likely to fund the project than if it's considering a project in airports that will primarily benefit the rich. We have baked into our rules a system that will tend to push money toward the rich and away from the poor, at a time when you think it's really important that the poor be able to make it to work in order to achieve economic mobility.*

"Infrastructure Week" has become something of a joke in Washington—leaders of both parties promise time and again to invest in the nation's infrastructure systems, and then never actually do it. Yet for those focused on doing something for the middle and working classes, this is the lowest of low-hanging fruit, and so we ought to do it quickly and without delay.

A massive push to renew and expand the nation's infrastructure may represent a lightning strike for those struggling to make it in today's America, but it's not necessarily a long-term solution. There is another endemic challenge, as Oren Cass argued succinctly: "We've essentially eliminated the pathways in the labor market that don't include getting a college degree, even though most Americans still don't earn one." Several conferees agreed that the only real way to address that challenge is to retool our education system. This emphasis on the benefit of work in and of itself illuminates for me one of the most important pathways out of the current darkness.

Ironically, Steve Pearlstein, who sparred with Cass in the opening hours of the conference, largely shared his opponent's view that the key to fixing the labor market is to reengage individuals and families who have been left behind. He offered two key suggestions: "Do something about early childhood education to make it universal. And do something about having an education system that doesn't try to channel everyone to college—but is much better at training people for the jobs that we really have, and the skills that they require."[45]

Glenn Hubbard, who served as chair of the Council of Economic Advisers for President George W. Bush and was the dean of Columbia Business School, argued that the crucial element too often overlooked when trying to tackle this challenge is community college. As he put it:

> *Community colleges are the workhorses in training. They are also successful in many parts of the country in partnerships with businesses in skill development. We need to radically change our support for community colleges. [Economist] Austan Goolsbee and I put out a proposal in an Aspen Institute study to have a new Morrill Act, like the land grant college movement that President Lincoln had championed.[46] This version focuses on public investment in community colleges to increase the supply of those college-educated workers and to promote midcareer skill development.*

We know these sorts of interventions can work because they *have* worked. As IberiaBank Corporation president and CEO Daryl Byrd explained, "South Carolina embraced technical education in the '60s, somewhat ahead of their time. Greenville, when I was a kid, was not too pretty a place. It was a textile town—or a mill town, as you'd call it in South Carolina—and they lost much of the textile business. But the community came together." He went on:

> *You've got a couple of good universities in the area, and you had a really good technical school, and then community leadership decided that they would go out internationally and try to attract manufacturing to the city. They were successful—Michelin tires and BMW. They have some chip manufacturers in the area. But it took some vision,*

*focus, leadership, and a thing that we seem to lack in this country
today: collaboration. Because these were public-private endeavors.*

And Belle Sawhill argued for a focus on the third leg of what might
be considered the nation's three-legged educational stool. Beyond early
childhood and secondary education, she advocated for the private sector
to take a much more proactive role in producing the workforce their businesses demand. "The business community used to invest in training, and
they don't anymore," she asserted.[47] "We do need to, somehow or other,
incentivize the business community to go back to training their workers.
They're the ones that know what skills are needed. They're the ones that
can help people move up the ladder as they gain the skills."

My own view, some of which I articulated at the conference, is that
there's actually much more we can do to address these challenges in offering free or very affordable tertiary education. Where in the Ten Com-
mandments does it say that free education should end at secondary school?

It also strikes me that, in the short term, Washington should elim-
inate the payroll tax. Established during the Great Depression to fund
Social Security and Medicare, the payroll tax has become perhaps the most
regressive element of the federal code—a charge on work that targets those
in the working and middle classes. The nation's economy would be better
off if we replaced it with a carbon tax, a value-added tax, an energy ineffi-
ciency tax, or really any other levy that doesn't penalize work.[48]

Focus on Smart Regulation

Second, we should set aside the endless (and often pointless) debate about
whether the financial sector needs regulation, and instead focus on culling
regulatory burdens down to smart regulation. The "pile" most borrow-
ers receive at any mortgage closing amounts to a ton of paperwork that
no ordinary homebuyer reads or understands—and the expense of producing it is a drag on the system. The same is true across the economy.

Washington ought to establish a National Institute of Regulation whose mandate it would be to work with the private sector in clearing out the diktats that serve only to hamper economic growth and prosperity.[49]

Ultimately, however, the challenge can't be tackled exclusively by the public sector. Businesses, which too frequently put shareholder profit above everything else, need to play a more proactive role in spreading prosperity, because whatever the short-term profit loss of doing something, the long-term cost of doing nothing is much more severe. In this regard, the recent, courageous, and somewhat controversial step taken by the Business Roundtable to urge companies to move away from the exclusive use of shareholder well-being to measure business success is of transformational importance.

Consumers, employees, communities, and shareholders all need to benefit from a growing company's success. Government can incentivize good behavior, providing some marginal cost savings when executives decide to put the greater public interest first. But ultimately, businesses need to realize it's not good for their bottom line if the people living in places like York, Flint, and Albany are left destitute and without hope of climbing the economic ladder. We need to prioritize both long-term and short-term policies designed to create a fertile environment for business success and expansion. In the end, the private sector will be the engine for most of the good, solid jobs of the future.

What does that mean for policymakers? It means they need to make a series of important choices and investments. For example, while the private sector needs to begin investing much more heavily in green technology, the public sector needs to make those investments more attractive to a business executive worried about profit margins. The jobs created by improving energy efficiency almost certainly redound to those who have been upended by the transition to an information economy. If more businesses provided charging stations for employee cars, installed solar panels on their roofs, and began purchasing electricity from renewable energy producers, jobs would open up for a different worker demographic.

The city of Boston has led the way on this by mandating that all major developments be LEED certified, meaning they "are planned, designed, constructed, and managed to minimize adverse environmental impacts; to conserve natural resources; to promote sustainable development; and to enhance the quality of life."[50] Other localities ought to do the same. If the United States led the world in green energy, we would lower energy costs, increase exports, help save the environment, and maybe most important, create globally competitive, sustainable jobs. And if the public- and private-sector efforts figure out a workable strategy, like the one Byrd described in Greenville, fossil fuel–producing areas will avoid being left behind.

Revitalize Opportunity Zones

Third, as several conference participants argued, businesses need to lean in to the opportunity zone program, an approach to revitalizing distressed neighborhoods that has existed for decades, but that has more recently been expanded and updated. Opportunity zones offer executives a simple bargain: If a business invests in a designated locale, it gets a tax break. As studies have shown, in some cases, those incentives aren't sufficient; in some others, they're too generous.[51] But as Mary Miller noted in a back-and-forth with Belle Sawhill, beyond perfecting the calibration, municipalities need to squeeze more benefit out of these programs, enhancing transparency and coordination between investors and local community leaders.

Invest in Scientific Research

Fourth, America should begin investing in basic scientific research again. Through the course of our recent history, public money (awarded most often to researchers at the country's incredible network of universities) has spurred innovation that, when eventually applied to commercial innovations, has driven economic growth. Taxpayer resources funneled to the Defense Advanced Research Projects Agency, NASA, and the National Institutes of Health, among other organizations, have proven over time to return much more to the economy than they drain from the federal budget. If communities left behind by the past waves of technological innovation are going to have a fighting chance in the future, they will need opportunities to harness the power of tomorrow's inventions.

A Ray of Hope

All too often in today's public discourse, pundits exclaim that we're living in "unprecedented" times. It's certainly true that the challenges we face today are different from the challenges humanity has faced in previous eras. But by that standard, we're always living in unprecedented times, if only because history never repeats itself precisely.

No one disputes that the changes wrought by technological innovation and global interconnectedness over the past two generations have sparked upheavals in our nation that are incredibly rare in recent history—and possibly novel in the history of American civilization since the colonies pried themselves free of King George III. But even if we're in unfamiliar territory, the recent upheavals certainly do compare with previous moments in history. We need to learn from those moments—what some societies did to harness the potential of the circumstances they inherited, and how others tripped themselves up by turning in the wrong direction.

As a college student at Haverford, I majored in Spanish literature. Since graduating, and through the course of my professional career, I've often thought about the world the Spanish inherited after Columbus discovered what was, for Europeans, a "new" world. (Of course, it was not new to those who already populated the continents and islands on the Atlantic Ocean's western edge.) By some measure, that moment and the more recent dawn of digital technology, set broadly five centuries apart, inhabit much the same amalgam of hope, fear, disruption, and possibility.

In both cases, a society found itself on the precipice of a new age full of unimaginable possibility. And in both cases, that shift sparked a great deal of fear, setting up a confrontation between those who wanted to lean in to the change—and those who wanted to turn away.

On the whole, the Spanish turned in the wrong direction. In the decades after the Spanish state financed Christopher Columbus's venture across the Atlantic, the Spanish ruling class failed to make the most of their good fortune. Rather than investing in what the Americas might eventually become, they chose to pillage their "discovery." While none of the European colonial powers was above exploiting the people and land they found across the Atlantic, Spain was particularly pernicious in seeing the New World as little more than a source of gold. And the Iberian Peninsula suffered for centuries for that lack of vision. The French, the British, the Dutch, even the Portuguese all invested in these unfamiliar lands, making the most of what was undoubtedly a lucrative economic opportunity. Spain, by contrast, just tapped its colonies for money to spend.

But that wasn't Spain's only mistake. Faced with a growing and perhaps overextended empire, the Spanish chose not to enrich their culture with new ideas and traditions, but rather to turn inward. Spanish Catholicism became rigid and exclusive, even to the point of alienating the Pope. Rather than integrating with the wider world, the Spanish sealed themselves off, building fortresses rather than commercial ventures. Some in Spain were aware of the mistake—Cervantes's *Don Quixote* was among the picaresque novels written to criticize Spain's frightened ruling class for mishandling the country's opportunities. But fear prevailed, and as history would eventually prove, Cervantes and the other critics were right.

America is at a similar crossroads today. We have at our fingertips technology that may make the discovery of the Western Hemisphere look insignificant by comparison. And while some of us are eager to lean in to the possibilities opened up by innovation and entrepreneurship—finding new ways to tackle climate change, pandemics, poverty, fraud, space exploration, and more—others, threatened by seemingly inevitable changes that will come as the world adapts to its new potential, are tempted to turn inward. The impetus to deny scientific facts, reject climate change, turn against immigration, raise tariffs, vilify technologists, and lionize a fanciful vision of yesterday's America is the most significant threat to the country's future prosperity. We need to reject it.

If we intend to benefit from our discovery—or at least not to squander our advantage à la sixteenth-century Spain—we need to build the bridges separating American communities from one another. As Yale Law School professor Jonathan Macey argued at the conference:

> There is compelling evidence to show that the provision of public goods—and I would include national health insurance and education in this category—suffer under conditions where voters are uninformed and polarized, because politicians in polarized societies rarely internalize the society-wide costs and benefits of their decisions. Politicians are trying to benefit increasingly narrow segments of the population rather than a very broad group.

If people living in York, Pennsylvania, and those living in New York, New York, share no common interest in the other's prosperity, they're both likely to suffer. The future of America's working and middle classes hinges on how we address that challenge.

A highly respected conference attendee, Nobel laureate and Yale economist Robert Shiller, focused directly on this point during his remarks. "The elephant in the room is the gradual forgetting of World War II, which was a nightmare and brought us all together," he avowed. "The primary determinant of our redistribution is not observations of inequality—it is wars. In a wartime, a different spirit develops . . . As that's forgotten, we're moving back into a normal state, which is much more combative within our society." And that's our primary problem. Few moments in American history have had the potential to be so prosperous. Rarely have we been so clearly at the precipice of such possibility. But at a moment of what should be abundant optimism, too many Americans live in despair.

As demonstrated by the substance of the conversation that follows, America has the tools and levers required to usher struggling and despondent communities back into the mainstream of prosperous society, whether in places like York, Flint, and Albany . . . or blocks from the nation's most prosperous creative capitals . . . or somewhere in between. But a salve will not emerge on its own.

The ideas bandied about in New Haven provide what is perhaps a blurry picture of where we need to head. I look forward to diving deeper and providing sharper contrasts, with new, fresh research. I thank all the participants and excitedly invite everyone with an interest in these issues to engage on this crucial topic in the months and years to come.

Opening Remarks

GENE LUDWIG, *Founder and CEO, Promontory Financial Group*: To begin, let me say a word about Heather Gerken, the Yale Law School dean. The dean of the Yale Law School has historically been a distinguished scholar, lawyer, and leader of enormous consequence. Over the last twenty months, we've been lucky to have Heather Gerken lead the law school. She is certainly among the strongest law school deans we've had, among very capable people—some would say the strongest law school dean in decades. She has brought new vision, energy, and commitment to the law school as it enters a different world. She really needs no introduction, but she's such an exceptional human being and intellect that it's appropriate for her to open the conference, because she's really the convener here, not me.

HEATHER GERKEN, *Dean and Sol & Lillian Goldman Professor of Law, Yale Law School*: That was way too nice an introduction. I have to say that Gene may have a little bit of a dean in him as well.

I know that everyone is really itching to dive into this conversation, so I want to just take a few moments to welcome you here before I turn it over to Gene. For many of you, I know this isn't your first time coming to Yale. We often have the privilege of bringing major figures—scholars in

American life—to speak to our community. But this event is something special. In this small room, we have some of the nation's finest economists, political figures, legal scholars, and business leaders. Collectively, this group has centuries of experience pondering and tackling questions of economic equity. Your colleagues here include those who have interacted with issues of income growth at every level of government. Some of you are mayors, fighting the basic impact of poverty and wage stagnation daily. One of you is a former governor who tried to expand the pie while balancing budgets. Many of you are alumni of the White House, Treasury Department, and Federal Reserve who have wielded the most powerful monetary and fiscal instruments in periods of growth and crisis.

We need all this intellectual firepower here today. Gene has laid out an extraordinary question before us: How do we address the stagnation of America's middle and lower classes before it's too late? There may still be some in the halls of government, business, and the academy who deny that the dividends of prosperity are uneven or that they must be a priority. But as they fiddle, the voices of men in action grow even louder.

I'm so proud that Yale Law School is the site for this amazing summit, because it is entirely in keeping with the traditions of this school. Lawyers grapple with inequality's consequences every single day, but they tend to deploy a fairly narrow range of tools in their efforts. Here, we try very hard to think big and dream bigger. We encourage our students to look beyond the existing tools. Today, we have a chance to interrogate long-held orthodoxies regarding markets, fiscal and monetary policy—even the relationship between elite institutions that all of us represent and an economic system that is not working for many. That is exactly the kind of intellectual courage that we try to cultivate at a place that stands at the intersection of the academy, professional training, and public leadership.

And luckily, we are led in this effort by a man who has a long track record of intellectual courage: our friend Gene Ludwig. So many of you already know Gene from one point or another in his storied career. He is one of the best examples I can offer to my students of how a career grounded in rigorous training in the law turns into a lifetime of service. After graduating from law school in 1973, he joined the D.C. law firm Covington & Burling, where he was a partner. His career took an extraordinary turn in 1993, when then-president Bill Clinton appointed him comptroller of the currency. Gene made it a priority to breathe new life into morbid statutes. For the first time, the Office of the Comptroller of the Currency began referring cases of lending discrimination to the Department of Justice, and he successfully cajoled banks into massively increasing their investment in community development projects. Gene told me yesterday that the things he is most proud of are the places where there was a fight and he stood strong. After leaving the Clinton administration in 1998, he put his expertise in financial regulation to use in the private sector. Rather than joining a bank or a fund, he decided that he could be most helpful by enabling institutions to comply with the regulatory system that he had helped build.

Gene founded Promontory in 2001. Since then, he has brought many of the nation's top regulators to work with him. His firm's wild success is a testament to his leadership and the depth of his team's expertise in one of the most important and complex regulatory structures in the world today. All the while, Gene continues to work on the core public problems that have long animated his career. We continue some of that work here today in a Yale clinic that bears his name and honors his legacy. That clinic is led by Professor Anika Lemar, who is here with us today.

Somehow Gene has done all of this while simultaneously helping the country understand market events and where we are in the world. He's written op-eds and reports; he's made countless television appearances; and of course, he brings people together for events just like this one. Sometimes people talk about Yale's extraordinary convening authority, and it is extraordinary. But we have nothing on Gene Ludwig. He has become a public intellectual, not for the sake of being known, but to force us to consider the world as it is, and as it should be. I know that all of you are here for two reasons. The first is to engage with one of the most challenging and important questions of the day. But the second is Gene. We all know him for his decency and integrity, his luminous intelligence, his ferocious work ethic, his courtliness, and his kindness. Many people wish that they had a career as storied as Gene's, but all of us aspire to be the kind of person that he is. With that, I introduce our real convener, Gene Ludwig.

LUDWIG: We're here together at an enormously important moment in history. The underlying fundamentals may be different, but the economic circumstances of today *feel* in many ways like the late 1920s. With the threat from China, the worsening trade wars, it *feels* as though we're on the precipice of another Smoot-Hawley [Tariff Act] moment. Europe is weak, the United States is very fragile, and we're burdened in Washington with a political system that clearly is not working.

This is a fraught moment, so let me try to frame what this conference is designed to accomplish.

First, I want to level-set the situation we face economically here at home. I'm personally outraged by some of the statistics you'll find in the reports we've compiled ahead of this gathering, and I'm frequently angered that we have not done more as a society to address the suffering many Americans endure every day. Take one statistic as an example: As of January 2018, almost 92,000 Americans were homeless in New York alone, with close to 3,000 family households sleeping on the streets.[52] That's sinful. In a society as prosperous as ours, no one should be sleeping beneath residential buildings where apartments run for $100 million.

Moreover, in a society that prides itself as a beacon of social justice, African Americans should not face an incarceration rate more than five times the rate of whites,[53] and African American men without a high school degree should not wake up each day to a reality in which nearly 70 percent are imprisoned by their mid-thirties.[54] To my mind, for that matter, it's outrageous that for every $100 a white family claims in wealth, an African American family has just $5.[55] But this is the reality of today's America—and it shocks the conscience.

At the same time, if those abject examples represent clear and present moral outrage, something else is going on as well. Economic inequality is at a breaking point, and it's a risk to the broader economy. As an increasing share of studies have revealed, the vast income inequality that defines America's broader economic profile is outrageous and unsustainable in and of itself. And it's not just activists beating the drums on this issue anymore. A number of business leaders, including Ray Dalio and Andrew Tisch (whom we are lucky enough to have with us today), have made this point and brought it more into the public consciousness.

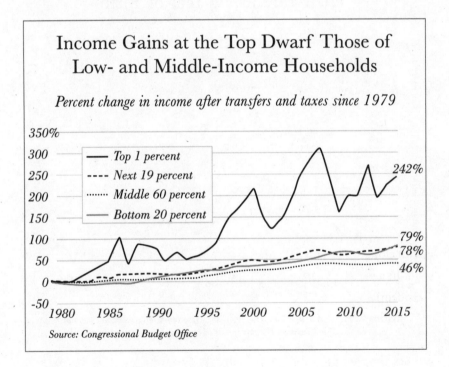

Income Gains at the Top Dwarf Those of Low- and Middle-Income Households

Percent change in income after transfers and taxes since 1979

Legend:
— Top 1 percent
---- Next 19 percent
······ Middle 60 percent
— Bottom 20 percent

242%
79%
78%
46%

Source: *Congressional Budget Office*

But I want to take a pause here and, having acknowledged these challenges, point your attention to something slightly different. Historically, many in our country have viewed the American Dream, amorphous as that term may be, as the centerpiece of our economic thinking. Because people believed that their lives could be better than their parents' lives, many of us haven't been so worried—or as worried as people in other places in the world—about income inequality *per se*. Unfortunately, however, if you look today, both in terms of the surveys on expectations and the actual numbers, it appears that this next generation's lives will not be better than their parents' lives, and could be much worse.

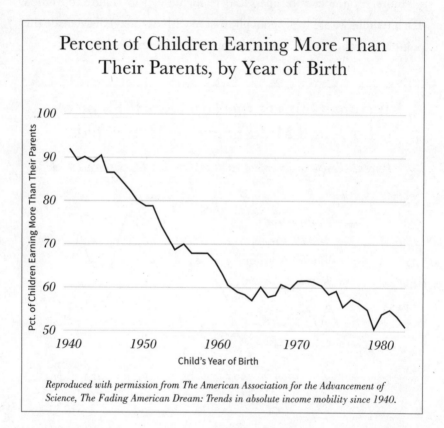

Percent of Children Earning More Than Their Parents, by Year of Birth

Reproduced with permission from The American Association for the Advancement of Science, The Fading American Dream: Trends in absolute income mobility since 1940.

In other words, poverty, prejudice, and inequality have always been a part of America's reality, dispiriting as that may be. Generation upon generation have failed to resolve those sins, let alone make amends. But the American Dream, inasmuch as it was attainable by some portion of the population, provided a rational reason for many to keep faith in the American system. And because that dream has become increasingly unattainable for a growing portion of the population, we face an entirely new challenge.

For this conference, we're focusing on economic circumstances beyond the narrower lens of income equality—a topic that has become, for good reason, a central thrust for those [who are] debating politics and policy today. Instead, we mean to have a broader discussion of the economic realities for middle- and lower-income Americans, irrespective of the widening gap separating their circumstances from those at the very top of the income pyramid. Some in the room may say that the gap itself really is the issue, and that will be interesting to hear. But I think the less frequently debated issue, in the context of the American Dream, is whether middle- and lower-income people can improve their circumstances regardless of where they began.

Now, everyone in this room is more expert about answering these questions and giving us pathways out of the swamp than I am. And many of you are more expert with the data than I am. Having said that, I've worked with a team of economists here at Yale and in my office over a whole year to compile the data set you have in front of you. Anyone who has read the spectacular books and articles that many of you have written will have some sense of the snapshot these statistics are designed to provide. But simply leafing through the numbers before you will pay dividends if only because they provide a kind of specificity beyond any broad strokes.

Some of these figures suggest we're facing the kind of situation we had in the late 1920s, as I have just [indicated]. Our economy has grown 20 percent over the last ten years, but 40 percent of American workers earn less than $15 an hour. Many find educational opportunities, health care, and, in some cases, housing beyond reach or almost unattainable. While the official poverty rate is 12 percent, some 40 percent of Americans don't have $400 to deal with an unexpected emergency, for medical bills or car repairs.

Note that this is at a time when we are told GDP is growing rapidly. These are *supposed* to be the good times—the boom times. And yet we *still* have this kind of economic difficulty. Which raises a crucial question: What is going to happen when we face the inevitable economic downturn?

Official Income Poverty Rate vs. % of Americans That Cannot Cover $400 Emergency, 2013–2017

50%
47%
46%
44%
41%

15%   15%   14%   13%   12%

2013   2014   2015   2016   2017

—— Income Poverty   ---- Cannot Cover $400 Emergency

Source: Bureau of Labor Statistics and Federal Reserve data

Here's another important statistic: Consumer borrowing is at an all-time high, almost $14 trillion. When you set home mortgages aside, you find that the rest of consumer borrowing is also at an all-time high, of $4 trillion—with auto lending at a sky-high $1.3 trillion.[56] I ask again, what's going to happen in a downturn? Who is going to repay all this debt? And how does that roll through our society and the global economy as a whole?

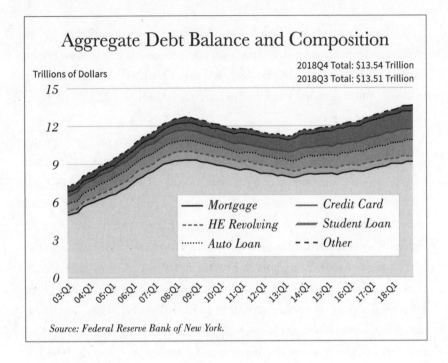

Aggregate Debt Balance and Composition

2018Q4 Total: $13.54 Trillion
2018Q3 Total: $13.51 Trillion

Trillions of Dollars

— Mortgage   — Credit Card
---- HE Revolving   ⚡ Student Loan
······ Auto Loan   --- Other

Source: Federal Reserve Bank of New York.

When I travel to York, Pennsylvania, where I grew up, and to towns around the country—when I visit community and regional banks—it often feels like we're on the edge of a precipice. I went to a public high school in a suburban area of York. Back when I was a kid, net-net, my school was a little less down-and-out than the city high school; it was reasonably prosperous. Today, when you go back to that same suburban high school, a third of the kids are on assisted lunch. Note again that my high school drew from what was considered the "wealthy" area of York.

We don't use our eyes and ears enough; irrespective of the economic aggregates, what matters more is what you feel and see and touch. And if you go to York—and I was back there to give a speech recently—it's immediately apparent that people are worse off today than they were just a few decades ago. And life there appears to be deteriorating even further.

We've done more than simply put together a booklet of charts and statistics. To get a handle on these issues, we have also compiled a table full of books authored by each of you. Almost everybody in this room has written an important book or article on relevant topics. I've read every one of them since we started this project, and they're fantastic. The scholarship you've all put together is magnificent, and together they will help point us out of the swamp.

I want to say a word about the folks who have been on the bleeding edge of public service. Luke Bronin, the mayor of Hartford, Connecticut, will be here with us today. Larry Summers was secretary of the US Treasury and director of the National Economic Council. Deval Patrick, who is our keynote speaker, was governor of Massachusetts and head of the civil rights division at the Department of Justice. And Sarah Bloom Raskin has been a regulator in Maryland, a Federal Reserve governor, and deputy secretary of the Treasury. I feel like the balloon act at the circus when they say something about my former role as comptroller of the currency. These are all folks who have seen policymaking and policy malpractice up close and personal and have tried to do something meaningful to make it better.

Back to the issues at hand . . .

A big part of this problem we face today is born from the state of the statistics themselves. Unemployment and GDP growth, for example, are reported monthly and quarterly, and those singular figures have an outsized role in defining the country's understanding of the broader economy. The markets can sometimes go wild simply on the basis of those two aggregate statistics. It is completely nuts that the statistics that, as a practical matter, would speak much more authentically to the reality most Americans face on the ground are not readily available to those who need to understand the true economic reality. What are most people earning— and what are they earning by geography and ethnicity? What are they earning in real terms, in respect of what they need to do to achieve the American Dream? What's really going on in the rest of America?

Beyond income disparity, dozens of key statistics are not readily available, and others that *are* available do not get the consideration they deserve. These statistics are so important in understanding day-to-day reality in America; they make the aggregates almost meaningless as a practical matter.

These are my impressions, my research, and my passion—the views of only one person. To really form a better sense of the objective truth, I invited you all here today to engage in a broader discussion among experts who have looked at these questions closely.

Accordingly, our first panel is extremely important. Speakers have been asked to grapple with the question of how bad things really are—and why.

Our second panel takes the facts explored by panel one a step further: What are the national-level solutions to the problem?

Our third panel focuses on the local solutions to the problem. There are those who believe that only national solutions work, and there are others who believe national solutions won't affect a broad swath of America's great diversity of communities. We need to weigh the options and perspectives.

Finally, I am hopeful that what comes out of the work of our three panels today will be used to make a difference in people's lives as well as to advance our collective scholarship. For example, I hope the Ludwig Center for Community & Economic Development will be able to take action. Glenn Hubbard, dean of the Columbia Business School, is here, and I hope he will offer some ideas for ways that Columbia and other universities can breathe new life into the American Dream.

You are policy leaders, and having at least the scholarly and policy community better know your views will add value. We hope to keep in touch throughout the year and have another symposium about this time next year. Why? We're getting into an election cycle. If we can find consensus between left and right on ideas that we think would help, we may well have an opportunity to make a difference. I'm hopeful that you will make suggestions of ways in which we can really move the needle—things that we haven't thought about but that really could turn the dial.

Now, let's get started.

First Panel

How bad off economically are middle- and lower-income Americans, and why?

During the 1992 vice-presidential debate, Admiral James Stockdale, Ross Perot's running mate, began by asking: "Who am I? Why am I here?" The line took off like a lead balloon, eventually establishing itself as one of the more memorable gaffes in recent national debate history. But embarrassing as it may have been for Perot and Stockdale, the quote applies rather aptly to the symposium's first panel. The discussion turned on an exploration of what was actually happening in the American economy in early 2019: Why was it happening? And (to a lesser degree) why hadn't policymakers done more to enhance the prosperity of middle- and working-class American families?

No one disputed that things are worse for those living nearer the margins. And while some were focused on the economic chasm that has opened between places like York, Pennsylvania, and New York, New York, a much greater share of the discussion hinged on the underlying causes of economic turmoil that broader aggregates so frequently obscure. On this point, everyone appeared to agree: GDP, aggregate growth, and unemployment figures—all of which, in 2019, looked better than rosy—do not paint an accurate picture of what's happening on the ground. And if the underlying circumstances are more dire than many appreciate, the question quickly becomes: How bad has it gotten, and why?

The discussion in the first panel was particularly lively, largely because the participants came from a broad range of perspectives. There is little need to summarize the various points of view here, but the transcript that follows reveals that there were heartfelt disagreements about the root causes: Is technology the root cause? Or, as some suggested, is the problem simply that government has not adapted to the economic changes wrought by both technology and a range of other upheavals? Regardless of these disagreements, the statistical and anecdotal descriptions of what is happening in much of America were heartrending. No one tried to defend the status quo.

CR

GENE LUDWIG, *Founder and CEO, Promontory Financial Group*: Let me just start by saying who's on the first panel. I'm not going to give their complete bios, which are extensive and impressive.

Oren Cass is a senior fellow at Manhattan Institute and an important author. His book, *The Once and Future Worker*, is out of this world, and I highly recommend you read it.

Jacob Hacker is a professor of political science at Yale and a very fine author. His book *American Amnesia* is also not one to be missed.

Andrea Levere leads Prosperity Now, an organization that collects as much information as possible on the real problems in America.

Steve Pearlstein needs no introduction if you read *The Washington Post*. He is a noted columnist and obviously an important public figure. He also is an author of a great book in this area, *Can American Capitalism Survive?*

Belle Sawhill is a senior fellow in economic studies at Brookings. She recently wrote a must-read book, *The Forgotten Americans*.

Let's find out how bad it is. And with that, let me start with Andrea.

ANDREA LEVERE, *President, Prosperity Now*: I just want to say what an extraordinary opportunity and gathering this is. What you don't know, Gene, is how responsible you are for what I do with my life. I went to the Yale School of Management, a couple of blocks away, which set me on my path focused on economic opportunity and justice.

I'm going to start with key findings from the Prosperity Now Score-card. We've been putting out the Scorecard for over fifteen years. The Scorecard has comprehensive data on how well the states and cities build and protect the wealth of their residents. We disaggregate this data by race, gender, disability, and geography. I hope Mayor Luke Bronin of Hartford comes in, because I've also included data on both New Haven and Hart-ford; it tells a stunning story. And I have to say that I never imagined the data on Hartford would look like it does.

Just to begin with the story that Gene has been telling us for the past two days, one in five jobs in the United States is low-wage. But this new element, which I think many of you have followed, is the impact of income volatility on households, and how that is a huge driver of finan-cial insecurity. Anybody who hasn't read the book *The Financial Diaries*, which tracks the issue of income volatility, should do so. It's an incredibly important supplement to the issue around wages.

For the first year [of the Scorecard], we have data on who pays their bills and who doesn't. And we found that 13.2 percent of households fell behind on their bills, and those with volatile incomes did so twice as much. We've pulled this out by race, and I'm going to be sharing this data throughout the presentation. A quarter of Black households have fallen behind on their bills. I'm not going to share the credit score data today, but this obviously has a huge implication since credit scores determine the cost of capital for these households.

One of the most important data points that we created for the Scorecard was a measure to assess household financial insecurity to complement the measure of income poverty. We developed, with an economist, the metric of liquid-asset poverty, which measures the ability of a household to withstand financial shocks. Liquid-asset poverty determines whether the household has enough savings to exist at the poverty level for just three months if their main source of income is disrupted—such as if someone gets sick or someone loses a job. The amount of liquid savings is very modest. It's $6,257 for a family of four. Forty percent of US households are liquid-asset poor.

Here's the local data: 31 percent of Connecticut households, 51 percent of New Haven households, and 63 percent of households in Hartford are liquid-asset poor. When almost two-thirds of the people in your city are looking at a state of financial insecurity, it constrains profoundly what they're able to do. When we look at this by race, we find that 63 percent of Black households and 63 percent of Latino households are living in liquid-asset poverty. This compares with white households that are 31 percent liquid-asset poor nationally.

Gene asked us also to break it out by quintiles of income, and this split is what I think is interesting. Even as you go up the quintiles of income, you see a significant level of financial insecurity. And this was true during the government shutdown, when people couldn't believe that government employees would go into food banks after missing just two paychecks in Washington, D.C. When the Scorecard came out the week after the shutdown ended, the liquid-asset poverty data captured exactly why government employees—with middle-class salaries—could suddenly be plunged into financial need.

The other key issue we look at is Federal Deposit Insurance Corporation data on who is unbanked and who is underbanked. Again, this data has profound consequences. If you look at the United States, a quarter of the people, basically, are financially underserved. Then you look at New Haven and Hartford; almost half of the residents are financially underserved. *Unbanked* means you have no mainstream financial account, while *underbanked* means you have some mainstream account but use alternative financial services. Mehrsa Baradaran, a professor at the University of Georgia Law School, documents in her book *How the Other Half Banks* that on average, a financially underserved person spends $2,400 a year on fees and interest. When I present this data, I always project how much a financially underserved person could increase their financial security if they could actually save even half of this amount spent on fees and interest.

Then we talk about who gets credit and who does not. This is a new data point that the Federal Reserve is collecting. About 20 percent of households in 2018 did not use mainstream credit at all [in the last year]. They often resort to payday lenders, and the Consumer Financial Protection Bureau (CFPB) payday rule that we thought was coming is no longer coming. This rule [would have] formalized the ability to repay debt as the standard for being able to qualify for a payday loan. That's raising all sorts of issues as we think about operating without any regulation for this type of lending.

The major source of wealth for American households typically is homeownership. Because of the whole foreclosure crisis, the rate of homeownership has dropped over time. [Now] it's rising again in the United States. In Connecticut, there are extreme disparities in homeownership, and we track this by every state and by cities. We look at who is able to purchase a home and what that means for their household net worth and the equity that they have. Yet you can see how similar the numbers are between New Haven and Hartford.

Then we look (and this comes back to the number Gene was citing) at median family wealth by race and ethnicity. And you can see, in fact, how dramatic the difference is—slightly different numbers, but telling the same story of the profound disparities in wealth between white households and Black households and white and Hispanic. This is not getting better, and we have multiple studies that document this. It would take 228 years for African American families, if their household wealth continues to grow at the rate it does today, to equal the wealth of white households today.

Some of the most provocative data to come out documents that education is *not* the great equalizer, which we have talked about given the great wealth disparities that students start with when pursuing education. The St. Louis Fed has done some of the most important research about the benefits from education in terms of household wealth and how this inequality affects access to and use of debt and future income.

Yet it is important to note that this new data affirms that people are still better off with a college degree—but the impact is not uniform. Looking at the disparities between what that means over the longer term for household wealth just affirms that there is no single solution to any of this. We have a whole set of solutions. One of the things we do with the Scorecard is present solutions that can address issues affecting housing financial insecurity and wealth.

We have a whole set of policies, some of which we shared in two documents with you, that have been implemented at the state and national levels and have shown direct benefits. We look at these policies in six categories: income supports, emergency savings, higher education, retirement savings, homeownership, and consumer protection. We are deeply engaged in expansion of the earned income tax credit (EITC); I'm sure we'll talk about that today. We also strongly advocate for building rainy day savings and children's savings. We run a national initiative for every child in America to start with a child savings account, to change their aspirations for college and their household, known as the Campaign for Every Kid's Future.

OREN CASS, *Senior Fellow, Manhattan Institute*: It's a real privilege to get to present to this group. I'd like to start with what I think is the most fascinating map I've seen from *The New York Times* in a long time. They took every county in the country and shaded it by the share of personal income in the county that came from government transfers. They showed what that looked like in 1975, and it was sort of a light beige, pasty map representing roughly 10 percent to 20 percent. Obviously, Social Security is going to be a large piece of that. Then they showed it in 2015, and it looked roughly like a measles outbreak. Outside of coastal metro centers, the entire map had become a medium to dark pink with bright purple. In some counties, the majority of personal income is now coming from government transfers.

The reason I start with that is, I think there are two ways to look at that map. One would be to say that it represents the greatest policy success of the last forty years. That is, in fact, exactly the economic model we pursued, which is to say that we are going to grow the economy as quickly as we can and redistribute from the winners to the losers. The darker the map gets, the more redistribution we're doing. The other way to look at it, of course, is to say that this is a complete disaster and represents exactly the central challenge facing the country. I think the latter explanation is the correct one. I suspect most folks anywhere on the political spectrum would agree with that.

I start there to emphasize that when we talk about how bad off economically people in America are, the problem is not material living standards. Every way of looking at the problem (that I'm aware of) shows that in terms of material living standards, virtually everybody at every socioeconomic level is dramatically better off today than they were in past decades, and certainly than they were in the so-called golden age of the '50s, '60s, and early '70s. That goes for access to a variety and quality of consumer goods and technology, [and] for their actual consumption levels after you take government transfers into account. Frankly, it goes for their health, their access to health care, and their life expectancy, notwithstanding (obviously) the various serious problems we've had in just the last few years. It goes for education. It goes for the share that complete high school, the share that go to college, and the share that complete college.

I think it's very important in having this discussion to focus not on material living standards—that is, how much we have succeeded in transferring to people. I think the actual problem is their labor market outcomes. What has happened structurally in the economy and in society is causing an ever-larger share of the population to be unable to actually find work that allows them to support their own family.

That's what has actually changed. I think it's the change (which is getting worse) that we need to focus on, rather than point-in-time statistics that may look concerning but have always been concerning, and are in fact less concerning than they have been.

Labor market outcomes have taken an extraordinary turn for the worse over the past thirty or forty years. Particularly for men—particularly for those without college degrees. The most striking way to see this is just to look at median earnings for a man with a high school degree and compare it to the poverty line. In 1975, a typical man with a high school degree could support a family of four at more than twice the poverty line. The comparable man today can only clear the poverty line by less than 40 percent. That's the difference between about the $34,000 a year he's earning and what would be $55,000 a year if he had kept pace with that threshold. That gap, I think, is incredibly important.

To Gene's point of getting beyond the aggregates: For young people in particular, labor market outcomes have gotten much worse. If you look at 25-to-34-year-olds, for instance, the share earning less than $30,000 a year has gone up from a quarter in the '70s to more than 40 percent now. That is including folks with college degrees. If you were to look specifically at those without college degrees, the picture would be even more dire.

It seems to me that the central problem we're having, and the one that then feeds into a lot of the statistics we just saw, is that people can't actually find jobs that are going to allow them to support their families, to build careers and wealth over time.

The other dimension is family and community health, which is not strictly an economic question, but ultimately it has incredible implications for both welfare and households. And it is economic in the sense that . . . Take savings and the ability to survive a disruption, for instance.

Historically, the model by which families would do that was not to tap a large savings account; it was to rely on the family and community in which they lived. And when you take those things away, you have a much more serious problem. If labor market outcomes and family and community health are really what has gone wrong, it is a serious problem.

I think it's important to emphasize that these things are sort of our fault, and there are things that we can do about them. I think there's a narrative out there that says somehow this is a function of automation or irresistible economic changes. The next data point I would emphasize is that none of this is a function of automation. We measure automation in our economy very carefully, by measuring productivity growth. We measure how much more we are able to do with fewer people over time.

Productivity growth has been slowing for a very long time and is currently at its lowest level on record, I believe. It's not that we're replacing people faster than ever with machines. It's that we've created an economy in which the types of jobs in which less-skilled people can work productively are less available than ever. We've essentially eliminated the pathways in the labor market that don't include getting a college degree, even though most Americans still don't earn one.

The last piece, which goes to the family and community point, and which I hope we will talk about, is one particular function of inequality. It is not the absolute difference in incomes, but the extraordinary residential sorting that we've seen. What has happened in lower-income communities is that they no longer also have higher-income households in them, which has effects on human capital, social capital, and networks. In terms of community strength, I think this has been incredibly damaging to the prospects for struggling Americans. That is something that has changed, that looks nothing like it did even at a time when we had much lower material standards.

STEVEN PEARLSTEIN, *Author and* Washington Post *Columnist*: It's an honor to be here with real scholars. I'm just a kibitzer. I was trying to think if I could boil down the problem to a sentence. I couldn't do that, but I did [boil it down] to two sentences:

> *Because of globalization, technology, deregulation, and changes in business norms, the benefits of economic growth have largely been captured by people at the top. The result has been—for most people, I think—an unacceptable increase in inequality of income and wealth and therefore opportunity, which has polarized our politics and rendered our government dysfunctional to the point that it now threatens our prosperity and our democracy.*

That's as succinct as I could make it.

I think around this table there's probably some fair agreement about that. I don't think we lack for research or data, and I don't think we lack for ideas about how to address this problem. Oftentimes, these kinds of conferences end with what further research needs to be done. I don't think so. I think we're pretty good on that score.

The problem is leadership at the political level and the business level. And to some degree, the problem is also followership: We don't have people who are willing to follow leaders anymore, and that's a problem. And it seems to me that what we need to do is sort of break a very vicious political cycle that's gone on, much like the Hatfields and McCoys, where one bad deed begets another.

You see this playing out every day in Washington, where I live. Just this week, the Democratic House couldn't pass a budget because the left wing of the party wouldn't agree to a simple budget outline. This process doesn't even appropriate money; it just gets the budget process for the year going. And it has totally broken down. We haven't had a budget for years, and what happened? Well, first, all members of the opposition party—in this case, the Republicans—vote against it. And then enough people at the fringe of the party in power vote against it so that it can't pass. So the resolution is withdrawn, and we do nothing. The party in power doesn't allow the other party to make amendments. At the committee level, the party in power over the committee doesn't consult with the party that is not in power on the committee. So nothing gets done.

To me, when we have these kinds of conversations about this issue, it gets a little frustrating because we do know what to do, and we just don't have the institutional ability to act on that general consensus. We can't get political leadership that's willing to sit down and solve the problem. They would rather have an issue with which to win the next election than actually solve the problem. If that's the reality, then it's hard to see how to proceed; the game has been played out to a bad political equilibrium. I think we could randomly select any twenty-five Americans, put them in a room, and tell them not to come out until they have some things to do that would make things better, and it wouldn't take very long at all. And that first step would give us the confidence to take a second, and then a third—and rebuild the trust that has been lost [but] that is essential for a political system to reach compromise.

I think we could all agree on a fairly simple set of ideas that would break the cycle and push us in the right direction:

- Expand the EITC and make the child credit refundable and bigger. There is wide agreement on increasing the minimum wage nationally to $10—maybe not $15, but $10 is a lot better than $7.25 and could be accepted in places in the country where the cost of living is a lot lower.

- Have a commitment from the business community that every business shares profits with its employees, which ought to be the norm.

- Do something about early childhood education to make it universal. And do something about having an education system that doesn't try to channel everyone to college, but is much better at training people for the jobs that we really have, and the skills that they require.

- Have a tax system that raises from corporations the same percentage of GDP in tax revenue as the Organisation for Economic Co-operation and Development (OECD) average. Not more, not any less—just the same.

- Have an upper tax bracket that is no more than 40 percent, but is no less than 40 percent, either. Make sure that everybody has private health insurance and spends no more than 10 percent of his or her income on out-of-pocket expenses.

- Make sure that we enforce an antitrust law so that we don't have a large swath of the economy where people earn rents.

There's a mix of what Jacob [Hacker] calls "redistribution" and "pre-distribution" on that list. I think we might want to redistribute a bit more than we now do, but not a whole lot more. Our emphasis instead ought to be on pre-distribution, making sure that people's market wages are fair and sufficient.

I know there are some more conservative people around the room than me, and some more liberal ones. But I don't think I said anything that most of you couldn't live with. And the fact that we can't get to that is the problem. More than that we can't agree on the problems or come up with fairly straightforward solutions, it's that we no longer have effective mechanisms for making those collective decisions and trade-offs.

ISABEL SAWHILL, *Senior Fellow, Brookings Institution*: I think an awful lot of the data points have already been shared by Gene and others. We all know that intergenerational economic mobility has declined a lot for younger generations, from the studies done by [economist] Raj Chetty and his colleagues at Harvard. In case you're interested, when you adjust for family size, it doesn't look quite as bad as the Chetty indicator shows.

That's something we're working on at Brookings at the moment. We all know that income inequality has gone up hugely. We know that wages, especially for the less educated or less skilled, have been flat or declining. We know that employment rates have declined, especially amongst men. Now they're beginning to decline a little bit amongst women as well in the United States. And instead of being in the top ranks in terms of labor force participation, compared with other advanced countries, we are now falling way down in the ranking on how many people are working.

I address all of these problems in my book, and I also talk a lot about cultural anxieties. I was interested in the people who elected Trump. Was it economics or was it culture that got him elected? And I don't think there's any nice, neat answer to that. It's a mixture of the two, but they interact in complicated ways. Then we have all the political problems that Steve just alluded to, which I think are at the heart of the matter. As he says, we do know what to do. Even though there are diverse values or perspectives around this table, we could find a way forward.

Oren and I, for example, don't agree on a lot of things. He's to the right, and I'm more to the left. But we served for a year together on a working group—an American Enterprise Institute–Brookings working group—that came out with a report on the working class in America this fall. We had a lot of recommendations that we all agreed about. Oren and I led the charge on the issue that he already talked about, which is the problem of low wages, especially amongst the less educated, and the fact that they can't support their families. He and I are both in favor of some kind of wage subsidy to boost wages at the bottom. It could be an expanded earned income tax credit, but I think Oren and I both favor not so much an EITC as a credit that's based only on your individual earnings, not your family income. We can get back to that if anybody is interested.

The other thing that I can add to the conversation is the importance of getting out and talking to actual people who are living difficult lives. After I finished writing my book *The Forgotten Americans*, I had a survey research organization put together for me—six focus groups in three cities. I defined "the forgotten Americans" as people without college degrees and in the bottom half of the income distribution. We went to

Syracuse, Greensboro, and St. Louis. These were very rich conversations, and I have written an essay on what we learned. But let me give you a couple of the takeaways.

First of all, people talked about how they were struggling. At one point, I asked people, "What class do you think of yourself as belonging to? Are you middle class? Are you working class? Are you what President Trump called 'the forgotten Americans'?"

I always remember one woman who said, "I'm in the hanging-on-by-your-fingernails class." That really sums up the way a lot of them felt: very insecure. They felt very replaceable. They saw their jobs being contracted out. They didn't think it was hard to get a job; they didn't complain about that at all. The problem was wages and benefits. They talked about how their employers used to provide a pay package with benefits and don't anymore.

But these workers are not asking for government assistance. They have a really strong sense of wanting to be self-supporting. They do not want handouts; they do not like safety-net programs. They'd say things like, "Well, I know a lot of people on food stamps, and they're milking the system." Even though a lot of them are dependent on these programs themselves, they don't like them. They really want to be self-supporting.

Then we talked about government, and their attitudes toward government are so negative, it's scary. Absolutely scary. They would say things like, "Well, government is a joke." Or they would say things like, "We should send all of the politicians back to high school finance class. They don't even know how to balance the budget. It takes them forever to get anything done. They just can't ever do anything. They're out of touch with people like me." I got lots of those kinds of comments.

So, what do we do? I have all the usual policy proposals in my book, and I see my time is almost up. But I would come back to the fact that we really do need to get the political system working again. I have a few ideas about that, but there are others here who know more.

JACOB HACKER, *Professor of Political Science, Yale University*: I get to go last because I wanted to talk about politics, drawing on two recent books with my co-author, Paul Pierson. In addition to thanking Gene, I have to thank Paul. Belle has set me up extremely well, as has Steve, because I do think this is ultimately a problem of politics, though it may be a deeper problem than Steve is suggesting. Maybe I should say it more broadly as two problems of politics that are deeply linked to inequality. The first one we're writing and talking about a lot now is right-wing populism. The second—which we're not writing and talking about but should be—is runaway plutocracy.

Right-wing populism is not a US-specific phenomenon. I like to show people [an image] of the path of the eclipse over the United States when the full solar eclipse happened recently. It goes from where I grew up in Oregon down to where my relatives in Nashville live, and it bypassed us entirely. But what it didn't bypass was Trump counties, as the red here on the map suggests. Some people may think it means that the Republican Party is the party of darkness, but I would never say that. What it means is that if you drew any line across the United States, it would be mostly red. This is relevant to right-wing populism.

Then you have your familiar red/blue map showing not just the hues but also the size of the population. So, of course, there are lots of blue voters in urban areas, as the tall bars indicate. Right-wing populism is a story of non-urban voters in all the countries where it's happening. [In the United States,] those non-urban voters are central to the Republican coalition for a couple of reasons. One is they're over-weighted by our electoral system, so they're a good group to have. They allow Republicans to get outsized margins relative to their vote share in Congress. They help a lot in terms of holding governorship as well as in drawing districts. This also matters because we have seen this huge change. We have seen not only rising inequality across individuals but rising inequality across regions. Larry Summers has recently written about this in a great paper, "Saving the Heartland." Those areas are culturally and economically radicalized.

And they are a huge part of the political realities that are making it so hard to compromise.

If you look at the trends in the economy recently, that is problem one. Problem two: We've seen enormous growth in inequality, with the concentration of income and wealth at the very top. This has been a dramatic feature of the last generation. And it's mostly financial and nonfinancial executives who are in the very top tiers.

Now, this matters for a number of reasons, both economic and political. I want to focus on the political reasons. At the same time that we have this right-wing populism roiling our politics, we have a growing share of the money in politics coming from the very top. The top 0.01 percent of contributors now comprise almost half of total campaign contributions. With continued Supreme Court efforts to deregulate campaign finance, they will almost certainly represent a higher share in the future. And that's, of course, alongside the longstanding increase in lobbying. It reached its recent peak in 2009, but let's not think that the problem just disappeared in its wake. These two things together define a polarized politics of drift that exacerbates inequality and tolerates right-wing populism, because a lot of what these groups are trying to do is block regulation and other policies from happening.

Paul and I have written about why the business community is a lot less supportive of efforts to try to produce good public policies [than] in the past. We've seen a simultaneous rise of a radicalized right wing that is very much being driven by cultural and economic change, and a plutocratic policy coalition that's very much being driven by rising inequality. The combination of those two really defines why it's so hard for us to act.

I wish I had an easy solution. I think the obvious thing to say is that we really do need to bring back the moderate Republican tradition. [In presentations,] I often show a slide that shows the Democratic Leadership Council—all the key people who were members of this movement to try to bring the Democratic Party to the right in the mid-'80s and '90s. Then I show a slide that says at the top "Republican Leadership Council," and below that—it's just blank. There are simply no institutionally powerful GOP moderates at the national level today. That's a serious problem.

But I want to make a final point. What Belle said about trusting government is fundamental. It's linked up with the decline of the kind of effective organizations that once brought people into politics and helped them understand what was at stake. In thinking about how to address this—and I hope we'll talk about this—a big part of it is creating organizations that represent people not only in the workplace but also in American politics.

LUDWIG: It's now time for a free-for-all—for everybody around the room to address these issues and (a) ask questions or (b) share thoughts.

There's one thing that was unstated, but was indeed implied in many of the comments from this first panel: So why are we where we are? How did we go from a situation of relative political harmony, as late as 1993 or 1994—I was confirmed by a [Senate] vote of 99 to 0—to the contentious environment we have now? Today, nobody gets a unanimous vote for anything. And that's your unspoken reason for the breakdown.

What do others think? Why are we where we are, and how did it happen?

ROBERT SHILLER, *Professor of Economics, Yale University, and Nobel Laureate*: The elephant in the room is the gradual forgetting of World War II, which was a nightmare and brought us all together. The primary determinant of our redistribution is not observations of inequality—it is wars. In a wartime, a different spirit develops as people are dying heroically, and you knew people who died heroically. As that's forgotten, we're moving back into a normal state, which is much more combative within our society.

LUDWIG: Bob, you spoke, recently, about technology, and it was fascinating. You're going back and suggesting that every time there's a new technology, there are people jumping out windows and saying, "The new technology will take everybody's jobs."

What do others around the room think about what we've been living through? Bob or maybe Oren mentioned the redistribution effect as really one of the causes for why we've evolved the way we've evolved.

SHILLER: Oren made a very strong statement that it's not technology, but it's difficult to make statements like that. Economic theory of a very primitive kind equates the wage that anyone gets to their marginal product. Technology is changing all the time, and it's a very delicate equilibrium. I don't know how we can prove that it isn't technology that's playing a role in making inequality worse at this time. Ultimately, the economic theory in its simplest form equates incomes—wages—to marginal contributions of output. If you look at all the changes we've had . . .

For example, in the 1980s, there was an inequality scare related to word processing and the disappearance of the ordinary secretary. That has happened; we do our own writing now. How is that going to affect the marginal product of those people who were doing that? We don't know that it hasn't already had a big effect, and we don't know that it won't have a big effect. The economic theory says that it all depends on the technology that people of different skills will earn. And as technology changes, it will change the relative income.

PEARLSTEIN: I don't think there's any disagreement on the question of technology being a major driver in inequality. There might be some disagreement about whether it leads to permanent and long-term high unemployment. Our country's pretty good at making the trade-off between wages and number of jobs. We always seem to create the jobs, even if it means pushing down wages. Technology has caused some people to become very wealthy and have high incomes, and other people, low incomes. So the people who created the word processor are richer, and the people who used to type on typewriters are poorer. I don't think there's any disagreement that technology—it may not be the only cause or even the number one cause of inequality, but it's right up there, along with globalization.

HACKER: I disagree with that. I guess it matters as to whether you think that technology is creating pressures for greater inequality, with which I agree, or whether you think those outcomes are always similar. I think you would agree that the labor market, institutions, and democratic politics can mediate those effects quite fundamentally. It is worth putting on the table that the United States is distinctive in seeing a sharp rise at the top that is coupled with a sharp decline for the bottom half of the population. And there's dispute at the margin about this, but if you look at the data—the latest work that [economists Gabriel] Zucman, [Emmanuel Saez,] and [Thomas] Piketty are doing, with so-called distributional national accounts—the evidence is clear. Here's Western Europe [when looking at share of national income]: top 1 percent red, bottom 50 percent blue. [The bottom 50 percent have a greater share of the national income than the top 1 percent.] The U.S. basically reverses places. The bottom 50 percent goes from 20 percent to 10 percent [of national income], and the top 1 percent goes from 10 percent to 20 percent. That's a very different picture from Europe.

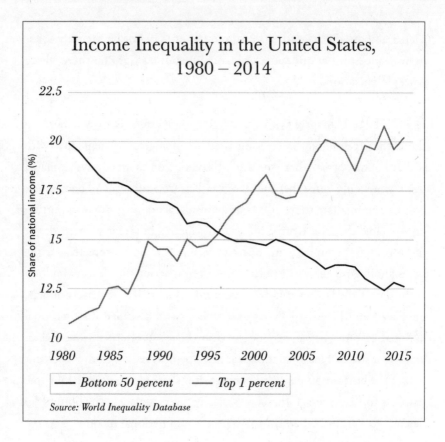

Income Inequality in the United States, 1980 – 2014

Share of national income (%)

— Bottom 50 percent   — Top 1 percent

Source: World Inequality Database

I do think technology is contributing to a polarized labor market. I was skeptical once, but it's become much more convincing. It's relevant to what Larry has been doing on regional inequality and what I mentioned about the radicalizing of working-class whites. Increasingly, if you look at population density versus wages, you're seeing that the lower end of the market now is not doing much better in cities, whereas it used to.

[Economist Enrico] Moretti and others have written about this. It used to be that cities seemed to have this kind of positive spillover, so that the lower-wage workforce was doing a lot better in the cities, which is a good thing because they have to do a lot better for people to afford to live in major cities. Now what Moretti shows is that there's basically no relationship between population density and wages for the lower end.

Which means that these folks are just in terrible straits, and the bifurcated labor market is happening. It's hugely important for our politics, and increasingly it's cleaving both parties. Even in those blue American cities, like Hartford and New Haven, a very large group of people are increasingly marginalized.

Just one last quick point, Gene, on your question about when it happened—I'm afraid in '94, the horse was at least starting to walk out of the barn. If you really want to date it, it has got to be the break of Newt Gingrich with George H. W. Bush over raising taxes in the 1990 budget deal, which gave rise to an anti-tax orthodoxy that got more and more intense on the right. It also gave rise to Newt Gingrich, who combined this kind of right-wing populism and appeal to tribalism with a plutocratic policy agenda. I think that's the moment when you start to see it: No Republican voted for the 1993 Clinton tax increase, which was in a balanced package that looked just like the 1990 deal that George H. W. Bush proposed. That's the kind of seminal moment, if we're going to date it. We were just very fortunate it hadn't hit banking regulation yet.

SARAH BLOOM RASKIN, *Former Deputy Secretary, US Treasury Department, and Former Member, Federal Reserve Board*: This data presents us with another problem, which goes to the question of resilience. Given what we've just heard, what is the ability now of the economy writ large to withstand exogenous shocks wherever they come from? Once a shock hits, and perhaps moves the trajectory of the economy downward, how long do we stay down? This idea of resilience is affected by some of the things Belle was saying in terms of people's distrust of government. Indeed, we see even now as an after-the-fact reflection of the financial crisis that there has been a weakening of the ability of policymakers to respond to a downturn, which then can contribute to and exacerbate a prolonged downturn. This is the idea of resilience: If we have a downturn, is it going to be a *V*, or is it going to be an *L*? Does the weakening of the household play a factor?

SAWHILL: There's a question about the resilience of individuals—but more important, the resilience of the political system—to manage the shock.

RASKIN: Both. But what you've brought forward are what I would call fault lines in the resilience of the household. We know that if households don't trust government, and if they don't have the economic means to bounce back from a shock, how in the world do we get out of any kind of downturn? Will it be just a minor downturn that pushes us down and keeps us down? That's the other problem that we've got to deal with.

LEVERE: Can I just quote Jacob Hacker, whom I quote all the time? The shift of financial risk from institutions to households over the last several decades has dramatically changed the financial resilience of households, which then feeds into all the issues that we're talking about.

LUDWIG: Bob gave us an image of a political world that is tribal; absent a war, we tend to go into our tribal corners. Do he and others think that this is historic, or that it's worse now? I'd also love to hear whether one major change we've seen is a material deterioration in the business community—or rather, a cycle of the business community. Let me tell you what I mean.

York, Pennsylvania, as our town lore would have it, was the only town in America where no banks closed during the Depression. Why? Because it was a mixed farm/labor area. [But today] the local industries, many of which became famous—York Dental Supply, York Air Conditioner, York Barbell, Harley-Davidson, Edgcomb Steel, and the second-largest Caterpillar tractor plant in the world—are gone or struggling in almost every case. Now, that could be simply a cyclical phenomenon, where everything goes to California. It also could be a secular phenomenon.

The tribalism of American politics could in some way be because there are no jobs. I'd be interested in people's thoughts. Why are we where we are? You could say it's because of national tribalism that we had in every prewar period. Or you could say it's because we have a secular or cyclical event having to do with deterioration of industries in America.

LAWRENCE H. SUMMERS, *Charles W. Eliot University Professor and President Emeritus, Harvard University; Former Secretary, US Treasury Department; and Former Director, National Economic Council*: I want to say two things that are partially responsive to what you said, Gene. The first is that groups like this one have a theory to which we naturally gravitate—that inequality breeds resentment. There's more inequality and more wealth, and that's all true. We do need to reckon with the fact, however, that if you ask people what they have confidence in, they have more confidence in banks than they do in the government. They have more confidence in the health care system that we think is a failure than they do in the press. If you ask people, "Is the American economy fair?"—high school graduates are more likely to say yes than college graduates. This guilt theory of elites—there's a lot of it at meetings like this—has some problems with the actual views of non-elites, much as those kinds of views appeal to me.

The second thing is that we need to be very careful about romanticizing the past of the business community relative to the present. The business community was the decisive factor that preserved affirmative action in the Supreme Court. The business community has been very good, all things considered, on gay marriage. If you read [former GE chairman and CEO] Reggie Jones, who was the leading business spokesman of the day in the period running up to Ronald Reagan's election, it was straight-out stridency that would go beyond anything that you would be likely to hear today. We need to be careful about embracing some idea that we once had this great community, and today we have a greedy disease of a community.

There's also a tendency in conversations like this to romanticize small business. I once heard a prominent businessman say, "I don't understand why everyone loves small business so much. They're a bunch of people who cheat on their taxes, don't hire African Americans, and don't give health insurance to their people." This view that small business is somehow good and big business is somehow bad is not consistent with the actual experience of the people who work in both of those areas.

HACKER: Can I just respond to what Larry said? I hope I'm not in the camp romanticizing the business community. I wrote a whole book about how this community was a lot more positively engaged in the mid-twentieth century, in part because of World War II.

I do think there's been a change, but it's not really about the individual business leaders. It's more about the overall level of positive engagement. We have fundamental problems that you might call public-goods problems, with business organizations becoming more parochial and less interested in tackling collective problems. There are three big markers of that development, from my standpoint. One is the Business Roundtable. It was founded as an organization that was going to speak as the business community statesman. While it was pretty conservative, it did play that role in its early years, in the '80s. But it has become singularly focused on CEO pay and prerogatives in the last fifteen years. And it's among the most moderate business groups.

The second marker is the Chamber of Commerce, which has changed dramatically to be much more GOP aligned and conservative. The third is the network of conservative organizations around Charles and David Koch. Conspiracy theorizing of the left aside—the fact is that their network spends roughly what the Republican Party does on politics. I don't see the Koch brothers as very statesmanlike on these kinds of issues. I don't know whether we can go back, but I think it would make a big difference if business was engaged. Take Tim Cook's Apple, which speaks very well about a lot of the dangers that Trump poses. At the same time, he and Apple were hugely supportive of the tax cuts, which were not financed, hugely inequality-increasing, and therefore a big threat to a lot of the things that we've been talking about. There's an issue of priority setting; even progressive plutocrats are abetting inequality.

SUMMERS: We can nuance this. Your comments about the Chamber of Commerce are the same as my comments about small business. That's the same thing. You're right about the Koch brothers. You're probably right that there is some tendency toward more parochializing. Over the last fifteen years, I have had substantial issues with my colleagues at the Harvard Business School who are prone to glorifying any business that puts in a few solar collectors or invests in the school system of its headquarters city—to just giving a bye through the entire set of issues of lobbying for "rifle shot" tax provisions and the like. This theory in the business community is that we're going to do socially responsible things ourselves, but government is going to screw it all up. To delegitimize it and not raise revenue for government is a popular idea in the business community. That does have very considerable truth. I had some experience with the Business Roundtable in the early '90s, and a bit in the mid- to late '90s. It's easy to romanticize where they were then, and the rights revolution is not a trivial thing.

JONATHAN MACEY, *Professor of Corporate Law, Corporate Finance, and Securities Law, Yale Law School*: On the Business Roundtable—I've been involved with that group since the '80s, and they've always been highly parochial. They've been parochial about different things. Now it's executive pay. In the '80s, it was pro-greenmail, pro-poison pills, stifling, hostile takeovers . . . but equally parochial. If we think about a Donald Trump, or a Newt Gingrich and the Contract with America—we don't want to personalize this too much in the sense of saying that these people are opportunistic. They're simply taking advantage of or pursuing what they think is a political support–maximizing solution. It's a path to victory and consistent with what Larry is saying about small businesses. What has made this sort of behavior such a winning strategy?

I don't know. But as we try to push toward a solution, that seems to me to be something to think about.

DANIEL MARKOVITS, *Professor of Law, Yale Law School*: On the question of the business community, the first thing is to understand the business community broadly rather than narrowly. It's not just a matter of a particular number of CEOs; it's a broader way of engaging in large-scale capitalism. None of this has to do with individual virtue or vice; everything has to do with structure. A series of structural changes, including the revolution in management consulting, have transformed the American firm over the last fifty years. Firms have been able to strip middle managers out and replace them with new managerial technologies that concentrate the management function and managerial prerogatives at the top. Over the same period, business schools and other postgraduate schooling became the leading way of training elite managers. If one joined IBM in 1960 as a junior-level person, one could expect four full years of training, or 10 percent of one's career, to be 100 percent paid for as IBM-provided training. Today, most American businesses provide almost no training. That's been moved into universities and business schools. These are all technological innovations. We shouldn't limit our understanding of technology to algorithms and robots. These are inventions and new legal technologies, new managerial technologies, new social technologies. They have, once again, transformed the American firm.

What do all these innovations share in common? They have massively increased the productivity of a narrow class of extremely well-educated and elite workers. The lawyers, the financiers, and the managers who now monopolize the management function and run businesses have—by downsizing middle management and stripping upward mobility prospects from production workers—depressed the productivity of everybody else. At the same time, a series of parallel innovations that establish the modern market for corporate control have made elite managers accountable exclusively to owners and not to other stakeholders in the firms.

None of that has to do with anyone being malicious or venal. It has to do with a structural and technological transformation in the way in which this kind of capitalism is organized. That explains a lot of the transformations in what we call the business community.

LUDWIG: Let me follow up on a couple of these comments and see how you react. One way to look at the change in politics—the tribalism—is to look at the change in the Democratic Party. It had been a party tied in large part to the South but, because of its stand on civil rights, became a party of the North. The tribalism and unhappiness we're seeing now is perhaps a reemergence of the South as a political force, where there is a cultural distinction in terms of business approach.

I wonder whether what we're seeing is because of the shift from the moderate northern Republicans as the dominant force in the Republican Party to today's more conservative southern force in the party.

GERKEN: It's certainly true that the parties have coalesced into a much more coherent form in this country. But we see high levels of polarization in democratic systems that are quite different from our own, with quite different histories from our own. It's possible that this is a contributor, but if you're really looking at the deep drivers of [the problem], the odds are that it's going to be something that affects all the countries at the same time.

On the polarization piece, we talk a lot about Republican polarization as being the source of the problem. I am not sure if that's just a matter of timing. The same forces that have driven the Republicans to the right are just as likely to move the Democrats to the left. Primaries are a huge problem for both sides because only the high-information voters turn out. They're the most extreme, and they're highly dependent on money. It's another group that is highly polarized. The primary is a huge problem for everybody, and when you add that overlay of the effect of wealth on elections, that's another reason for it. We may just be seeing the Republicans going first, but it's quite possible that we're going to see the Democratic Party lurching to the left over the next five to ten years in the same fashion.

LUDWIG: On the one hand are the legitimate grievances on the part of ethnic minorities and women and the LGBTQ community, and on the other is the inability of older generations to digest that change. One way to think about this polarization is in terms of the dramatic change in society, which has caused people to rightly express their grievances more.

GERKEN: It's true that these controversies swirl all the time around us, but I am, like Daniel, more tempted by structural analysis on this front. The economic drivers of this are profound, and there are also political structures behind it. It's not just that we are tribal in the sense of being likely to align with one side or the other. It affects our reasoning. One of my colleagues, Dan Kahan, will survey people about something that they know nothing about. Imagine nanotechnology; the average American has no idea what nanotechnology is. [Yet] if you cue them politically, not only will people have a view about whether nanotechnology is a good idea or bad idea depending on [the partisan cue], but they'll invent reasons to explain the positions that they're taking, even though they don't know what nanotechnology is. The depth of polarization isn't just cueing votes; it's cueing the way that we understand the world, and that's a deep problem.

MARKOVITS: Gene, your question about the relationship between the rights revolution and diversity and inclusion on the one hand, and economic disputes on the other, returns to a theme that has come up several times. The rise of white nationalism in a segment of the population has lots of sources and is very complicated. But among other things, it is a reaction to the elite's embrace of diversity and inclusion. While driven genuinely by an idea of equal dignity of all people, this also serves the ideological purpose of laundering the elite's economic privileges. Institutions like the one we are in now can say, "We organize ourselves on the merits. We're fair, and we admit everybody regardless of background or creed." That makes it seem OK, in the minds of the elite, that it also captures an increasingly large share of economic surplus. The elite can say, "We're doing this in an honorable way." So the way in which meritocracy includes some people disguises the way in which it excludes other people. This makes it inevitable that some measure of the resentment from those who are excluded gets directed at the diversity and inclusion component of elite life. That's not to say that elites should abandon diversity and inclusion—values that are essential to making our society fairer. But it does call for sensitivity and moral humility in elites, who can tend toward pride and even smugness.

MACEY: On the issue of the rise of white nationalism, the points that Daniel and Heather were making are right. The caveat, though, is there's really nothing new about this phenomenon. It is exactly what we saw during the Reconstruction era. What's new or different is that it's happening on a much larger scale in the United States as well as on a global scale; a longstanding political equilibrium is changing here and in many other countries. Groups of white people who enjoyed a certain amount of political power, even at low-income levels, are feeling very threatened by societal changes, legally and demographically. It's giving rise to this kind of predictable reaction. The question, obviously, is what to do. But I don't think nationalism is surprising, other than the scale of it at this particular time.

JAY SHAMBAUGH, *Director, The Hamilton Project, and Senior Fellow, Brookings Institution*: On the broader question of why and what happened, there are two forces that I haven't heard us mention much that changed both the politics and the economic structure. One is the decline of private-sector unions in the United States. It changes the politics, because they play the big role in politics. It changes the training, because they used to play a big role in training. They're not there as much when you ask, "What happened to the wages of lower- and middle-income, especially less-educated, workers?" There was a political shift that allowed that to happen or contributed to it happening.

In addition to technology, [we've seen] shifts in the way trade has been working in the United States. The United States used to work where industry spawned, in high-education, high-innovation places, and then spread out across the country over time. You always had factories closing. The Yorks of the world always had factories closing. You'd drive around New Hampshire and see all the old mills that shut. They didn't shut to go overseas. They shut to move to South Carolina. You have got things spreading across the country to these places that now no longer seem to have as much. When we used to have trade shocks from Japan or Europe, they were hitting the high-education, high-innovation areas more. As the global economy has shifted now, the trade shocks are hitting the lower-education, lower-innovation places that have less ability to pivot. [Meanwhile,] the high-education, high-innovation places keep spawning industries, keep spawning more and more successful places and people.

But things don't seem to filter away, either, because of unions or because of the way trade is working. Those are both forces as to why this is happening in the way that it is.

MARY MILLER, *Former Under Secretary, US Treasury Department*: Most of what you talked about was the labor force implications of what's going on today, but we didn't talk about retirement security, which is one of the biggest looming crises in the country. I wonder if you have any thoughts about the implications—politically, economically—of large swaths of Americans moving into poverty in retirement. I talk to people who think they will have to work until they die, and I don't know if that will even be possible for them to do, given the changes and the types of jobs that are available today. I wonder if that issue isn't going to force our hand a bit in terms of policy. Oren, do you want to address that?

CASS: On the retirement question, it's an interesting illustration of some of these challenges because, of course, we have Social Security. People who have worked throughout their lives actually are entitled to arguably our largest government transfer program that's designed specifically to keep people out of poverty in old age. We can say that it's not sufficient, that it needs to be bigger. I'm not a Social Security expert; I don't know exactly who earns what. But ultimately it goes to the same point: that this is exactly the place in which we have created the largest, most generous, most direct cash government transfer. To the extent that people are feeling it's not sufficient is an important issue to surface. But I would be suspicious that, therefore, a larger package of payments to them is the right path to go down.

I have to be honest: It's a little bit surprising to see the extent to which a discussion about what is the state and why of lower- and middle-class Americans has become a discussion about broken politics and especially about what's wrong with the Republican Party. I am second to no one in thinking there's a tremendous amount wrong with the Republican Party, but the implication there is that if only we fixed our politics, we could then solve all these problems. I don't think that's the case at all.

The question about unions and trade was excellent and an important one to investigate. I agree with a lot of what [was] said about the effects that technology is having. At the end of the day, what I've been intending to communicate about technological disruptions is that it has always happened. It is happening now, certainly, but it's not happening faster now than it used to. What appears to have changed—and the resilience point put this really well—is that on the back end of that disruption, we don't have an economy that is generating new and better opportunities. The example of the difference between mills moving from New Hampshire to South Carolina versus just the business leaving is a really important one. Before we posit that *If only our politics functioned better, that would really tackle these solutions*, we need a much better theory of what has changed structurally and economically—and what we're going to do about it.

There are some things on Steve's list I agreed with, but I certainly don't think Steve's list is something that would reach broad-based agreement or pass [as legislation].

LUDWIG: Business communities around America are not generating the same kind of jobs they used to,[57] and that respect for work goes to your comment, Oren. I read your book, *The Once and Future Worker*. It is excellent and makes several important points. Whether someone is being paid a lot of money or a little, people really benefit from work. We are not according work itself enough respect, and that has affected the sense of well-being in the country as a whole.

GLENN HUBBARD, *Dean, Columbia Business School, and Former Chairman, Council of Economic Advisers*: I couldn't agree more about work. I'll talk about that in the next panel, but I want to go back to what Bob said about the World War II generation. It was an extremely provocative and interesting point. I hope we don't [have to] repeat World War II to bring the country together. The president may try to do so, but let's hope he doesn't succeed!

The question now is, are there things that can bring people across social and economic groups together, in a mandatory way? Much as military service did in World War II, is there something that might serve that purpose, short of war?

SAWHILL: In my focus groups, when I talked to people about national service and what they thought about the idea of asking every young person to give a year of either military or civilian service, and about maybe getting some educational benefits along with that, they were enthusiastic.

I also talked about what I call an American exchange program. This was a new idea that I tacked on to the old idea of national service, which is that if you served in a community that was not your own community, you would live with a family that would voluntarily open their home to you—hosting a young person much like in a foreign exchange program. They just loved that idea. They understood, in a way that was very different from those of us around this table, that we have become tribal and divided, and they're not happy about that. They saw this as a really practical and uplifting way to address that problem. I was very struck by that.

They really understand the need to rebuild skills. They understand, and they argued that not everyone should go to college. They understand that having a college credential helps you a lot these days. But they're resentful of the people they see in their own workplaces who have that college credential and who, they feel, don't really know as much as they do—because these are young people coming in without experience, without practical skills. [The people in my focus groups] really want to see a reemphasis on vocational and technical training; they see community colleges as the path to doing that. Not elite universities—they're quite resentful of the elite universities. When Oren and I were working on this joint project on the working class this past year, one of our recommendations was to reallocate attention and even resources among everyone going to college, and to provide a lot more and a lot better opportunities for technical training.

The business community used to invest in training, and they don't anymore. Government training programs are not all that effective. We do need to, somehow or other, incentivize the business community to go back to training their workers. They're the ones that know what skills are needed. They're the ones that can help people move up the ladder as they gain the skills. That's something that we could also have agreement on across the political spectrum.

MICHAEL MOSKOW, *Vice Chair, The Chicago Council on Global Affairs, and Former President, Federal Reserve Bank of Chicago*: Talking about the broader question—what changes have taken place in our society—brings me to the word *household*, which we have tossed around here a great deal. Belle mentioned, at one point, that some of the data will change, depending on the size of the household, which is obviously true. But there have been enormous changes in households in the United States. The idea that we have two parents and two kids in a household is outdated. There are many more single-parent households today—no matter what ethnic group, no matter what religion, no matter what race. And I assume geographically it's true as well. Obviously, households are very important for kids; that's where all the interactions take place for them as they are growing up. But I would encourage us to be more specific when we talk about this term. When we present data, it will say that the data for incomes would vary depending on the size of the household. It's important that we take into the consideration these changes that are taking place in our society.

SUSAN KRAUSE BELL, *Managing Director, Promontory Financial Group, and Former Senior Deputy Comptroller, Office of the Comptroller of the Currency*: Before we leave the question of *How bad is it?*—I feel like we haven't really tried to size this problem. Many are saying that technology is changing the *distribution* of jobs more than the *overall number* of jobs. That makes sense to me. What's behind the very strong job numbers we have right now, and how could we size the problem of the people who don't have the right skills and aren't getting employed when we have this big labor market shortage? We can't put in place reasonable policies without doing a better job of trying to size the problem.

LUDWIG: What I'm hearing is that we cannot solve the jobs problem, the decent income problem, the middle-class problem if we don't have real private-sector companies that are employing people in higher-paying work. What I'm hearing around the table is that government transfers are only a Band-Aid; they're not a solution to people feeling economically insecure.

Is it a matter of reeducating in a way that makes it more possible for middle- and lower-income Americans to match with the good jobs that are available? Or are there not enough jobs available because of globalization and technological change? Maybe there are folks around the table who do know the answer, but I don't know the answer.

HACKER: I have two quick reactions. One is—and a lot of people have written about this—the decline in labor force participation in the United States, among men in particular, is a big deal. We used to have basically the highest labor force participation rate in the rich world, and now we're down in the double digits in terms of rankings. It's a serious issue. It's not universal, so it raises questions about why our policies are doing that.

The other point to make is that the quantity and quality of jobs are two very different things. The degree to which we're producing lots of bad jobs—or more precisely, low-wage, no-benefits jobs—is a fundamental part of the story.

LUDWIG: I'm glad you said that, because one of the saddest things is the lack of respect we have for people who do jobs that make our lives better. This drives me crazy. Many of us think of ourselves as professionals, but too few Americans consider somebody who is sweeping the floor by night a professional. Why? Shouldn't the lens through which we view professionalism be doing a job, whatever the job, in a professional fashion—by which I mean that they are performing a service or crafting a product with care and integrity? As we transition our society to a more service-oriented society, one of our big problems is both payment to those folks and our own attitudes toward those folks—[that is,] they don't think they're employed at anything worthwhile because the "elites" don't think of those as real, professional jobs.

PEARLSTEIN: There is a very simple model—I know it doesn't describe things in the golden days of the '50s and '60s, but it partially describes things: We had entities called large corporations. They used to train people because they figured those people would be there through their entire life, so it was a good investment. Another thing corporations used to do is redistribute income from high-productivity workers to those with less productivity. They equalized the distribution of income within the firm, so it was not [the case] that everyone was paid according to his or her marginal productivity. Young workers were paid more than their marginal productivity, while people at the height of their skills were paid less [than theirs]. Janitors who worked at IBM earned more than janitors in the open market. There was a compression within the firm. Then global competition came along and prevented companies from doing that.

The fact that people aren't [employed by the same corporation for] their whole lifetime means that everyone has to "earn" their marginal product—at least in theory. That has happened.

In other countries where we compete, they rely on the government to do the equalization in some way, because the firm, in a competitive market, can no longer take that initiative. We did the first part—end the internal distribution—but we didn't do the second part, the government part. There needs to be an acknowledgment of that, particularly by the business community. That doesn't mean they should all unilaterally go out and pay their janitors more even if that's not economically feasible. But when someone in Washington proposes some policy that might help equalize things—say, a change in the labor laws or the minimum wage, or requiring firms to share profits with workers—I wish the business community wouldn't make it its life work to block that policy.

We have a pretty long history of being able to deal with these problems, which has allowed us to maintain social harmony and social capital. We do not [have that ability] now. In a policy sense, we can't deal with even the simplest and most pressing problems.

Second Panel

What can be done at the national level to boost the economic well-being of middle- and lower-income Americans?

If the first panel was framed by Admiral Stockdale's quote from the 1992 presidential debate, the second panel was framed by a quote Andrew Tisch included in his remarks: the classic line from the Howard Beale character in the movie *Network*: "I'm mad as hell, and I'm not going to take this anymore!" Participants articulated a wide range of theories as to what might be changed nationally to help middle- and working-class Americans climb the ladder of prosperity. And interestingly enough, for all the vigor in the debate, reform ideas were focused not on any one social injustice, but on ways to expand opportunity across a whole range of sectors.

The sheer breadth of the discussion was remarkable. Panelists lobbed in ideas for national-scale solutions that ranged from higher education to unpaid work, and from infrastructure prioritization to smart regulation. Striking throughout the discussion was the sense that education has become an almost indispensable ticket to middle-class life. Education has always been a leg up—but during the Industrial Era, you could thrive without a high school degree. Today, by contrast, that's rarely the case. With that underlying reality in mind, most proposals sought either to (a) provide more Americans with the skills they need or (b) help those struggling without the benefit of such credentials to improve their condition.

Certainly, as nearly everyone agreed, the circumstances have become more dire in many parts of the country. But unmistakable throughout the discussion was a sense that policymakers and private/nonprofit-sector leaders still have cards to play. Certain challenges in public life may simply be too big for any institution to tackle. But here, in one room, were experts with a plethora of proposals that could and should be tried. Easy as it may have been to come away from the first panel with your head in your hands, the second panel highlighted a variety of potential action items that provide us at least some sense of optimism.

◌

LAWRENCE H. SUMMERS, *Charles W. Eliot University Professor and President Emeritus, Harvard University; Former Secretary, US Treasury Department; and Former Director, National Economic Council*: Our first speaker is Andy Tisch, who has been a leader in terms of business thoughtfulness and has given a lot of thought to these issues around the responsibility of business. His corporation has tried in ways consistent with business values to do a variety of things to make the world a better place.

ANDREW TISCH, *Co-chairman of the Board and Chairman of the Executive Committee, Loews Corporation*: Let me open with a quote that may be familiar to many of you. "We know things are bad—worse than bad. They're crazy. It's like everything, everywhere, is going crazy, so we don't go out anymore. We sit in the house, and slowly the world we are living in is getting smaller, and all we say is, 'Please, at least leave us alone in our living rooms.'" Now, the speaker of that quote is Howard Beale, and the movie is *Network*. Though it was released forty-three years ago, Paddy Chayefsky's words feel just as relevant today.

So many of our fellow citizens, especially those in the beleaguered middle class, share Howard Beale's feelings of anger and alienation. What does it mean to be in the middle class? It depends on whom you ask. It depends on where they live. It depends on how much money they make. It depends on a lot of things. But in many ways, middle class is really a state of mind.

I recall being in China—probably ten years ago, specifically on a Friday night, specifically in Xi'an. It was December 24, Christmas Eve, and we were going across town to go to dinner. I witnessed probably a half a million young Chinese men and women partying—subzero temperatures, everyone there celebrating, no inebriation, no intoxication. What were they celebrating? Who knew? Who cared? Our host said it was the new Chinese middle class, celebrating the fact that every year since their birth, they had seen their quality of life improve by 7 percent to 9 percent.

We certainly do not see that euphoria in our middle class. Decades ago, the middle-class mindset was defined by aspiration, by a belief that if you worked hard, you could buy a home, support your family, send your kids to a good school—and you could do it on one salary. It was called the American Dream. Today, the middle-class aspiration has curdled into anxiety.

All this as wages stagnate and both spouses go to work. The basic costs of living have spiraled upward. Family health insurance premiums and housing costs are growing twice as fast as workers' earnings. The cost of attending a four-year public school has tripled in the past thirty years.

While this has happened, the ratio of CEO pay to that of the average worker has grown from 30 to 1, in 1978, to 270 to 1 today. Is it any wonder that middle-class people are getting mad as hell and they're not going to take it anymore? The dysfunction and polarization in our government are both a cause and a symptom of this anger, because Washington's decisions and indecision have played a direct role in the decline of America's once-great middle class. It's a symptom because angry citizens are electing angrier and more intolerant candidates who see compromise as a form of treason. The vicious cycle is continuing; the middle class feels unwanted, unprotected, unappreciated, unloved, and abandoned.

Why has income stagnated in the middle class? One of the reasons is that for the first time in our history, one can create a significant amount of wealth without assets—and sometimes without employees. You don't need pipelines, steel mills, factories, or legions of employees to build a great company. You just need an idea. Very few middle-class employees are needed to sustain wealth. Look at Amazon—600,000 employees at minimum or lower wages.

Look at General Motors. At its peak, General Motors employed 850,000 people worldwide, 600,000 of them in the United States. The two largest companies in the United States by market cap today are Microsoft and Apple. These two companies combined employ less than a third of the number of people that GM once did. America's leaders in government, business, and elsewhere still don't know what to do about it. For too long, too many leaders have focused exclusively on today with very little regard to tomorrow.

Politicians do what they need to do to get to the next election, which typically involves peddling simple slogans for complex problems, and trying to divide rather than to unite. Companies do what they can to get to the next quarter. It's real short-termism. This approach is failing not only this generation, but the ones to come.

In business, there is a line item in every company's budget called maintenance capex. Now, capital expenditures for maintenance aren't sexy. When a company's finances are tight, they're the easiest to cut because the cost of deferral does not show up immediately—that is, until your ship turns into a rusting hunk of metal or the assembly line breaks down completely. Then the bill comes due, and it's usually much more expensive than it would have been if you paid for everything on time. Well, the bill is coming due for America's middle class. The bill for our future is coming due because of our failure to rebuild infrastructure . . . to invest in education . . . to properly fund Medicare, Medicaid, and Social Security. Trillion-dollar deficits as far out as the eye can see. It's just like businesses endlessly deferring their maintenance capex, and the bill is coming, which is why Gene has asked us all here today.

When Howard Beale made his primal scream forty-three years ago, it felt to many as if America was in a permanent decline. We were not. We rationalized our businesses. We rewrote our tax codes. We right-sized our federal budget to the point where we eliminated our national debt. Leaders in business and government made bold reforms, and American ingenuity was released to tackle the previously intractable problems.

What we need to do now is get mad as hell and not take it anymore.

SUMMERS: Bob Shiller has won the Nobel Prize in economics. What stands out about Bob again and again is his way of having a different idiosyncratic and successful slant on a whole range of economic issues—most famously, on the once-fashionable idea that markets are rational arbiters of value. This idea is held in much less repute today than it once was, because of—more than any other person—Bob and his work.

ROBERT SHILLER, *Professor of Economics, Yale University, and Nobel Laureate*: I am going to list some of the insurance- and finance-related efforts to deal with inequality. I was inspired by the work of Gustav von Schmoller, an economist in Germany in the nineteenth century. Around 1900, he wrote in his memoirs *Character Builders* that the nineteenth century was a great period for the expansion and application of the concept of insurance to problems facing society. He and others led the way for Germany adopting the first social security system, the first accident insurance, the first government-sponsored health insurance system, under [statesman Otto von] Bismarck. It wasn't Bismarck—it was the economists who did this. The important thing about carefully constructed insurance contracts is that they can help you avoid gratuitous inequality. We're not interested in taking the money away from a family that became a millionaire family by working fourteen-hour days in the family store for a lifetime. That's not what we want to take away. We want to take away that random, senseless part of inequality.

I wrote a book, *Macro Markets*, in 1993, about how financial markets can deal with risk to people or directly, and another one, *New Financial Order*, in 2003, and then *Finance and the Good Society*. I'm doing a very quick summary. History encourages me to think that these ideas are slow to develop. I don't get easily discouraged when people don't jump on these ideas. We still don't have national health insurance; that's over a century-long effort. The first principle I want to mention is what I call in my books "livelihood insurance." It could be privately offered, but the idea is that we want people to ensure their careers. When you get a Yale law degree, you could develop an insurance against people who get similar degrees showing a decline in lifetime earnings. This could help you reeducate yourself and make a transition, if it works out badly. Yale Law School does this already with the Koch program, but it's not done widely. This is another example of how slowly these things happen.

Another one is home equity insurance, which there have been several attempts to start. This hasn't been a success. But the idea is that your home might lose value, and that's the majority of most people's wealth. So, it should be protected. You buy an insurance policy—it could be in addition to your homeowners insurance policy—that ensures you against declines in the price of homes; a major protection against inequality. In the process [of writing these books], I did manage to succeed somewhat in establishing a futures market for a single-family home.

[The late economist] Karl Case and I created home-price indices that were specifically designed to be the settlement basis for contracts on home prices. In 2006, the Chicago Mercantile Exchange created markets for ten US cities, including New York and Boston, which are still going today.

Again, however, it's disappointing—it hasn't developed into a major market. But it is predicting a weakening of the housing market. Also, the options markets on single-family homes—we succeeded in getting that started, but it hasn't attracted attention. It's a very weak market. I don't get discouraged for the long term, because I think the real problem is there. It's going to happen to homes on the coasts when the sea level rises, if it does from climate change, and there's no plan in place to help people.

I just mentioned health insurance. That's not one of my innovations, but it's something that goes back to Germany in the late nineteenth century. It is an amazing development of modern civilization. Another invention—it's not mine, but I'm putting it on my list—is long-term property and casualty insurance. Right now, your homeowners insurance will adjust your rates as conditions change, but things happen to homes in [certain] regions. I mentioned global warming, but it's also things like hurricanes. There's nothing in your homeowners insurance policy to protect you against the possibility that there will be a whole new era of massive hurricanes destroying homes.

The critical point about the insurance of our time is that you have to deal with it before it happens. Let me also mention inequality insurance—insurance against rising inequality—which will be in our government program. It would be a plan to raise taxes in the future on the rich, if inequality gets even worse than it is today. I think that is more likely to succeed than doing it now. This is also [lawyer and economist] Ian Ayres's idea here at the Yale Law School—I call them "continuous workout mortgages." They have a preplanned workout. In the last financial crisis, we discovered that nothing was planned for all these people whose home price declined massively and who now have a debt greater than their home value. We should have mortgages that take this into account in advance.

Finally, international risk management—I'm surprised there is not much talk at all about what we will do if global warming requires massive migrations from one hard-hit region to another. There has to be a plan, some kind of risk-sharing across nations.

SUMMERS: The next speaker is Daniel Markovits, who has written proactively on a whole variety of aspects of law and public philosophy, and whom I have found most interesting as a critic of meritocracy.

DANIEL MARKOVITS, *Professor of Law, Yale Law School*: I want to start by fixing a particular account of the problem. In any economy, there are two kinds of inequality. There's low-end inequality, which concerns the gap between the poor and the middle class, and there's high-end inequality, which concerns the gap between the middle class and the rich. Historically in this country—when LBJ's Great Society got going, for example—the core problem was low-end inequality.

Today, the core problem is high-end inequality. You can see that the share of national income captured by the top 1 percent has roughly doubled in the past fifty years, even as the poverty rate as conventionally measured has fallen to between a half and a quarter of what it was at the middle of the Great Recession. You can also see, if you look at Gini coefficients, something extraordinarily striking. Separating out Ginis within the bottom 70 percent of the income distribution and within the top 5 percent reveals that inequality in the bottom 70 percent remains lower than it was in 1964, while inequality within the top 5 percent has skyrocketed. Indeed, there have been recent years in which the Gini within the top 5 percent has exceeded the Gini for the entire income distribution. So there is now more income inequality in the richest twentieth of the US population than in the population as a whole, which tells you how concentrated income has become at the top.

Moreover, the rich now distinctively work. Probably three-quarters of the increase in the top 1 percent share of national income over the past fifty years is attributable not to a shift away from labor and toward capital but rather to a shift within labor—from mid-skilled, middle-class labor to super-skilled, super-elite labor. The elite gets this income by working long, long hours. Among full-time, non-self-employed, prime-aged men, the bottom 60 percent of the income distribution now work nearly 20 percent fewer hours per week than they did in 1940. The top 1 percent now work about 15 percent more hours. In absolute terms, this is a shift of the labor effort away from the typical bottom-half worker to the typical top 1 percent worker of sixteen hours a week, or two regulation workdays.

The phenomena that we were describing earlier, importantly including technological change, are suppressing opportunities for middle-class work to a degree that approaches the extent to which gender discrimination suppressed women's opportunities for market work at mid-twentieth century. We therefore face maldistribution that distinctively concerns not poverty but rather wealth.

This story of how we got here focuses on a massive and historically unprecedented concentration of human capital—in particular, education and training—in a very, very narrow elite that is increasingly chosen on account of being children of rich parents.

To begin with, college graduates are marrying each other as they never did in the past and at such rates that there are very few college graduates left over to marry people who didn't graduate from college.

Next, education increasingly influences parenting. Historically, the chances of having a child outside of marriage were largely not determined by a person's education. Today, the bottom two-thirds of the distribution by education have over half their children outside of marriage. The richest 5 percent not only bear children within marriage, but they raise their children almost entirely within intact, stable marriages. These families then spend enormous amounts of resources on educating their children outside of school. The gap between top-quintile and bottom-quintile enrichment expenditures has tripled in the past thirty years. Within school, the gaps are even greater: The gap between a typical middle-class family's school education expenditure per child and a typical poor family's [expenditure] is roughly $5,000 a year. But the gap between a middle-class family's and an elite family's [expenditures] can reach $60,000 a year.

This produces massive differences in childhood achievement. Academic achievement, as measured by school testing, for middle-class and poor children has been roughly stable or even convergent over the past fifty years, even as rich children outstrip middle-class ones, in patterns that closely mirror income ratios. Moreover, these are very, very large effects. For example, by 2000, the rich/poor achievement gap had come to exceed what the white/black gap was in 1954, which is the year *Brown v. Board of Education* was decided. Economic inequality is producing differences in educational achievement today in the United States as great as apartheid did at midcentury. Moreover, the gaps again are principally rich/middle class gaps, not middle class/poor gaps.

These gaps endure as children grow up. On the SAT, the gap between the average score of a child whose parents make over $200,000 a year and [that of] a child whose parents make between $40,000 and $60,000 is twice as big as the gap between a middle-class child and a child at or below the poverty line. This produces the skewed elite. A child's odds of going to college and the quality of the college that the child attends both rise steadily alongside parental income rank.

At the most elite colleges, the skew to wealth is even greater. At the 150 or so most competitive colleges, kids from the top quarter of the income distribution outweigh kids from the bottom quarter by 14 to 1, and—in a way, more strikingly—outweigh kids from each of the middle two quarters by about 6 to 1. At the Ivy Plus colleges, there are more kids from parents in the top 1 percent than in the bottom half. At the most elite tip of the Ivy Plus—Harvard, Princeton, Stanford, and Yale—there are more kids from the top 1 percent than from the bottom 60 percent.

One way to think about this is to compare this way of transmitting privilege to the traditional aristocratic way, which was to give bequests of physical or financial capital to children on the death of their parents. Imagine that each year, you took the difference between what a typical 1 percent household spends on educating its children and what a typical middle-class family spends, and you put that into the S&P 500 and then gave it as a bequest to the child on the death of the parents. That would yield roughly $10 million per child. That's the extent of the intergenerational transmission of advantage through the mechanism of accumulated human capital.

Why do people do it? It is mainly that education has such enormously high social and economic returns today. Whereas there was basically no professional school premium or graduate school premium to wages in 1970, today someone without a high school degree has only about a 1-in-75 chance of earning as much over her lifetime as the median professional school graduate. Somebody with only a high school degree—that's roughly two-thirds of the population—has only a 1-in-40 chance of earning as much. Someone with only a BA has only about a 1-in-6 chance of earning as much as the median professional school graduate.

If we're interested in a solution to such inequality, we need to dilute this human capital at the top—and massively open up education, including elite education, to the broad middle class.

SUMMERS: Thank you for a very powerful presentation. Our next speaker is Sarah Bloom Raskin, who most recently served as the deputy secretary of the Treasury. She has been involved in financial regulation and the protection of consumers in one way or another for a very long time.

SARAH BLOOM RASKIN, *Former Deputy Secretary, US Treasury Department, and Former Member, Federal Reserve Board*: I'm going to attempt to be super pragmatic. There are three things that we can be doing at the national level to deal with what has been laid out as significant deviations from optimal prosperity. First of all, I'm going to talk about improving our measurements. Second, I want to talk about investing in priorities that have the highest returns on investment (ROIs). Third, I want to say something about how we do it, which is by giving states and localities great latitude to run pilots that produce results, which can be then evaluated and scaled up.

First of all, in terms of improving our measurements, Gene has laid out an important challenge here—that our measurements are not really giving us a full understanding and a full way to communicate the extent of the issues that we're talking about. I want to point out two particular macrostatistics that need to be added to the lexicon.

One is a Jacob Hacker innovation, the Economic Security Index. This is an index that is going to take a lot of the pieces—which Andrea [Levere] laid out so well and which Gene has laid out—and capture them in a macroaggregate. While it is good to have an understanding of these granular pieces, I think that if we want a data point that's going to compete with the top headliners of the unemployment rate and GDP, I think we need a macrostatistic. I'm going to advocate for a statistic that captures some of the fragility in the lower- and middle-income parts of our country. This could be the Economic Security Index; there are other candidates for it, but something like that would be a good start.

The second data point is looking at unpaid work. This is looking at the labor done by unpaid workers and is currently not part of GDP. When I talk about unpaid work, what is this? In developing countries, a lot of times it's hauling the water; it can be quite physical.

In the United States it is taking care of sick family members, washing the dishes, transporting the kids, caring for elderly parents. These are measures of productivity that are not captured in any way. We should think about how to capture them. We've got some good hints that this could be useful. The Gates Foundation has found that reducing women's unpaid labor from five hours a day to three hours a day could increase a country's female labor force participation rate by 10 percent. Thinking about how we bring into our metrics an understanding of unpaid work is a useful area to pursue.

Second, we should consider investing in priorities that have a high ROI. In this example, what I am seeing is investments in human capital. How do we evaluate various investments in human capital? This is something that begins to turn positive results in terms of higher pay and better employment. For example, there's a 13 percent ROI for comprehensive, high-quality, birth-to-five-years-old early education. This is not the childhood education that is in the headlines, which is, what do we do in the elementary school years? I'm talking birth to five years old. What do we see? We are seeing improved health outcomes. We are seeing improved social behaviors, higher pay, better employment. And we're also seeing reduced cost coming later in terms of health care and costs associated with poverty. This research comes from [economist] James Heckman, and it focuses on the life-cycle benefits of an influential early childhood program geared to the ages zero to five.

A study was done in North Carolina of poor African American children from ages zero to five—one model with excellent nutrition, fantastic day care, support for working parents, and early learning, and another model with the current state of childcare in that state. Children were randomly assigned to either the higher-quality resources or the lower-quality resources. Data is collected longitudinally—data points are taken through to adulthood. What has been shown are positive effects on high school graduation; positive effects on years of education, adult employment, and lower drug use; lower blood pressure and better health outcomes; and higher labor income. We see a two-generational effect. For example, mothers can enter the workforce, and their earnings can go up because their children are gaining the foundational skills necessary to put the mother at ease—as well as to make the children, as they develop, more productive in a future workforce. This childcare generation absolutely generates very positive ROI.

Finally, we should be running these studies locally. We need to think about piloting some of this work at the state level. Then, with good pilots in hand, we can compare ROIs and make credible policy recommendations.

ZACH LISCOW, *Associate Professor of Law, Yale Law School*: I want to take up the question posed by Gene, of how to sort among these surfeit proposals for helping lower-income Americans. I want to return to intellectual foundations. We economic experts should cool it somewhat when it comes to finding the most efficient solutions, as conventionally defined, to addressing these problems.

I'll describe what I mean. Let me begin with an illustrative example on infrastructure spending. Many of us in the room think it is important. As has long been the practice—including under President Barack Obama—when the Department of Transportation allocates money to projects, it does cost-benefit analyses to find the most valuable projects. The key component in that analysis is the value of time saved in transit. The current practice by the Department of Transportation is to value the time of the poor less than the time of the rich.

As a result, if the Department of Transportation is comparing a project—say, a bus line to help lower-income people—it will value the time of people less and be less likely to fund the project than if it's considering a project in airports that will primarily benefit the rich. We have baked into our rules a system that will tend to push money toward the rich and away from the poor, at a time when you think it's really important that the poor be able to make it to work in order to achieve economic mobility. How could it possibly be that even in the Obama administration we had a rule like this? How could it possibly be that we treat the poor so much worse, given that they're the ones who really need the transportation spending?

There is a core economic logic to it, to having this practice, even if you care about helping the poor, which is that this is efficient. It is efficient to spend a lot less on the poor to get them to work than to spend on the rich. The basic logic is that the economic pie grows more if you get the richer person to work more quickly, because that richer person earns more wages per hour than a poor person will earn per hour. The efficient thing to do—even if you really care economically, even if you really care about the poor—is to spend lots and lots of money getting the rich to work more quickly, grow the size of the economic pie, and then give cash transfers to the poor. Use tax and transfers to make everyone better off.

This is the system. This is the economic logic that we're very familiar with. That's what we teach undergrads; that's what we teach law students. This is the logic of the elites. Yet this logic is problematic, and it's incomplete. It often hinders good policy analysis.

I think that we should treat the rich and the poor equally, and that the problem with the standard economic logic is twofold.

First, I'm skeptical that this system will ever give the poor enough cash to make them whole, [to reach] equal treatment of the rich and the poor. Why am I skeptical that we'll ever give these cash transfers? Emerging evidence from carefully designed survey experiments in economics—as well as from decades of experience across the Western world, including countries that do the most for their worst-off citizens, like Denmark and Sweden—suggests that voters are more willing to get in-kind transfers like bus service than to improve a quality of opportunity. [They're more willing to ensure] the ability to get to work rather than to give out cash.

This plays on the very useful pre-distribution notion that Jacob [Hacker] introduced a decade ago, as well as the work that Oren [Cass] has been discussing. Policies like bus service, I suspect, are more socially acceptable because they tap into people's notions of reciprocity: You have to give to get. You have to go to work in order to receive economic benefits.

Second, as a matter of basic fairness, we should treat the rich and the poor the same. This speaks to the broader notion of indeterminacy on knowing what well-being is about. From where I sit, basic procedural fairness could be a really important thing to lots of people in the same way that encouraging people to work—having people working—could be an important thing for a lot of people.

Transportation cost-benefit analysis is just one example of a larger phenomenon: trying to find the most efficient way to do things. For the same reason that we might want to help poor people get to work with buses, maybe we should be open to a whole range of things that we might think of as less efficient: Providing childcare. Providing health care, which in many cases is not going to be efficient for high-cost individuals. Providing housing, perhaps—maybe greater place-based policies. Maybe funding these things with increased taxes on capital, which may not be the most efficient way to do it. This does not just imply liberal priorities.

Maybe we would be more open to well-designed work requirements for benefits programs.

These are all things that economists tend to take dimmer views of. Given my economics training, I've reluctantly come to think that we need to be more open to policies of this type. As we consider the long list of policies that think tanks in D.C. have put out and that we've been discussing today, I hope we're careful about our intellectual foundations, and that we consider important, widely held principles that are often ignored by economists, like equality of opportunity, notions of reciprocity, and basic procedural fairness. While establishing basic facts and doing careful analysis about efficiency, I hope that we're relatively open to what the democratic process produces to help lower-income Americans in ways consistent with these principles.

GENE LUDWIG, *Founder and CEO, Promontory Financial Group*: I'd like to say a few words about the one thing I know a bit about: regulation. A premise for my thoughts on regulation is that businesses exist on the margin. However successful or dominant a business is in its niche, competition eventually becomes fierce—and ever more international. The more you can make a business more efficient and effective, the more the business can grow and prosper. To the degree you cannot do so, the business can be competed out of existence. A business that is prosperous produces more and better jobs. One that declines does not.

Regulation can protect business in a variety of ways—by creating a marketplace for fair and safe business—or it can gum up business with overly bureaucratic and sometimes unneeded regulation. And by the way, when I say "protect business," this, at its bedrock, is about protecting the consumer and the marketplace. Business flourishes when it adds real value to real people. But for business to do this, regulations must add real value, too.

Most people confuse what I call "smart regulation" with deregulation, and that's a big mistake. Smart regulation is a shift that champions more effective and efficient guardrails. The new regime can stabilize markets, ensure that competition is fair, and protect consumers in ways that, in the end, benefit the underlying business. Sound business practices and marketplace integrity build business and competitive advantage for the broader society. Deregulation can be the willy-nilly elimination of regulations that may in the short run lower the cost of doing business for some or many businesses. But it can also create an environment of excess and excessive risk-taking that can, in the end, prompt business decline through low-end competition—or catastrophic decline through a tail event as we saw in 2007.

The Great Recession's cost to society, to businesses, and to low- and moderate-income Americans was enormous. America would be massively better off had we been able to anticipate the crisis and maintain regulation that would have minimized or avoided the impact. And in fact, better regulation at the time would have made a difference. At the same time, having been a regulator myself, I know that many regulations exist only because of history, not because of logic. Most regulations are not the product of academic or scientific rigor. Furthermore, rarely do regulatory agencies engage in a meticulous effort to ease any given burden.

You can't overstate this. While many regulations were well intentioned when written, they later have absolutely no basis other than somebody's long-obsolete whim in trying to do the good thing. They are never scientifically considered. No one weighs their utility over the long run.

Technology has given us a considerable opportunity to achieve positive regulatory outcomes that are less burdensome. An example is Global Entry and other programs designed to ease border entry. The controls are better, and it vastly decreases burdens. Electronic toll collection—E-ZPass—is another example of lessening a burden and yet achieving higher standards of collection.

Beyond the use of technologies, one can achieve increased effectiveness while greatly reducing any burden by avoiding regulatory duplication. In bank regulation, for example, every large banking organization today has multiple bank regulatory agencies to answer to—often with examinations by different agencies doing the same thing. There is no evidence that this overlap adds any value.

A third category where there is opportunity to lessen burden and increase effectiveness involves out-of-date regulations that can either be modernized; incorporated into existing, more modern regulations; or eliminated.

Fourth, we should be conducting, every several years, a regulatory inventory, with every agency engaging inside and outside experts to reevaluate the regulatory rulebook. This reevaluation should be organized to determine whether the existing regulations achieve the policy objectives to which the agency aspires. The reevaluation should assess which regulations could safely be eliminated or enhanced. Right now, we don't think about how to enhance them to make them more effective; we just think about how to pile one burden on top of another. We don't take the existing burden seriously.

Fifth, we need to increase the degree to which academic institutions have effective programs in the regulatory space. Perhaps we should have a national regulatory institute to increase academic rigor with respect to regulations in general.

Since 1863, banking regulations have done nothing but increase.[58] That's been the case in Republican and Democratic administrations alike. It just keeps increasing, and there's no reason to believe we're more effective for it. That is not to say banking regulation is not needed; it is needed for sure. However, for all the regulations upon regulations since 1863, we still had the 2007 debacle.

Some will say that improving our regulatory infrastructure is not the biggest issue for business competition and is at best tangential to middle- and low-income problems. I respectfully agree and disagree. Certainly, regulation is not the biggest problem. But if we don't grow our private sector, we won't grow good jobs. Without good jobs, we won't be able to provide better outcomes for middle- and low-income Americans. Being in business myself and advising banks, I can tell you that regulatory quality does matter a great deal to business competitiveness, as does safety. This is a highly competitive world, and there are only so many hours in a day. Waste is no one's friend.

As I liked to say when I was in government: Bigger isn't better. Better is better. Furthermore, a sensible regulatory atmosphere affects the animal spirit in all of us. As Bob Shiller and others would say, mood and attitude are immensely important—not just for the outcomes but for how people feel—whether they're willing to invest, take the risk, and move the country along.

In sum, there's much that can be done in the regulatory space to provide a better environment for business development in the United States while at the same time protecting consumers and the economy at large. This is an area in which the United States should lead, not follow. We ought to, as a nation, put a lot of more emphasis on this than we do.

GLENN HUBBARD, *Dean, Columbia Business School, and Former Chairman, Council of Economic Advisers*: As a moderate Republican, a southerner, and a business school dean, I am in all of the pockets here. I wanted to return to the earlier discussion of "work" in my remarks. This is an important thread in the discussion.

Scottish Enlightenment thinkers focused on mass prosperity. Much of what they meant by that was opportunities for work—not just the opportunity for an entrepreneur but for an ordinary person to take whatever his or her skills were and make something out of them. In Economics 101, we always say to students that technological change, free trade, and globalization improve economies on average. Gainers can compensate the losers, and that's what makes this discussion important in a political process as well—experience tells us that gainers have not really compensated the losers.

I want to focus on the compensation more in terms of opportunities for work instead of increases in non-work-related transfer payments. Economists are normally very suspicious of talking about people as anything other than consumers. We view work as having dis-utility in economics, but I would like to suggest a broader view that puts work back on the economic policy stage. I offer this point not to celebrate a person as a producer but to remind everybody that to get higher wages, you have to be on the ladder of work to begin with.

There are externalities to the loss of work—in health, in drug addiction, and in social pathology. There are three things to do to address the concern about it: growth, preparation, and support for work. I will focus on preparation, but first I'll remind everybody that growth itself is not the enemy. It still works. If you go back to the Obama administration's 2015 *Economic Report of the President*, you will find a fascinating discussion: If we return to productivity growth's halcyon days of 1948 to 1973, that return is more meaningful for a typical median worker than returning to a "more favorable income distribution." Growth matters, and it matters a lot.

On support, we need as a nation to increase quite substantially our support for work—through an expanded earned income tax credit. Focused at least as much on childless workers—the code words for "younger people coming up through the system"—I would add to that EITC expansion personal reemployment accounts that I and others have championed for a long time. I see those support mechanisms as dominating universal basic income in increasing incomes of low-skilled workers. [These accounts] are focused on work itself.

Going back to preparation, I want to highlight two areas for further inquiry. The first is an expanded role for community colleges. They are the key institutions for helping enhance skills for work for many individuals. Higher education is more than just Yale, Columbia, and Harvard.

Community colleges are the workhorses in training. They are also successful in many parts of the country in partnerships with businesses in skill development. We need to radically change our support for community colleges. [Economist] Austan Goolsbee and I put out a proposal in an Aspen Institute study to have a new Morrill Act, like the land grant college movement that President Lincoln had championed. This version focuses on public investment in community colleges to increase the supply of those college-educated workers and to promote midcareer skill development.

Austan and I had two goals and estimated a price tag. The first goal related to the decline in funding of community colleges per pupil per year relative to four-year state schools in almost every state. We wanted to close the completion gap that exists between two-year college students and their four-year peers for the eighteen- to twenty-four-year-old population, by increasing that completion rate from 37.5 percent, which is where it is now, to 60 percent by 2030. We would do that by equalizing funding between public two-year and four-year institutions on a per-pupil basis.

The second goal addresses other Americans ages twenty-five to sixty-four: to increase the share of Americans in that age range with a college degree or another high-quality credential from about 46 percent, where it is now, to 65 percent by 2030. We didn't pick 65 percent randomly; that figure was the expected share of jobs—according to economists studying it—that would require advanced skills by that year. We think that these proposals could be built with strong accountability mechanisms, and we would do it as a temporary program through 2030.

Some obvious first-dollar investments would include student support and advising, financial incentives that support course and degree completion, and improved remedial education. The cost of doing these initiatives, by our back-of-the-envelope revenue estimates, would be about $20 billion a year. Is that a large number or a small number? Certainly, it sounds like a large number. But relative to many training expenditures and the size of the problems we are talking about, I don't think it's that large. Importantly, what we are *not* talking about is a financial aid expansion. This is not the free college movement. This approach harkens back to Lincoln's intuition in the Morrill Act—the importance of increasing the supply side of skill development.

A second piece in preparation is working with the business community. IBM has not gotten heartless; if it reduces training, it is likely adapting to a different labor market where it no longer holds people for their [entire] career. Spillovers in training represent an externality. A firm can train somebody who then goes to work for someone else. We know how to deal with externalities: We can directly subsidize training. And we can encourage partnerships with local community colleges. The partnership, for example, that Toyota entered into in community colleges in Kentucky was not simply to be a good citizen. The partnership helped to develop a supply of skilled workers for Toyota.

In terms of funding these initiatives, the obvious spending offsets would be through reducing current federal support for training programs. Another potential offset comes from progressive reduction in old-age benefits. Can we do more for younger people? Is this the right time? I'd remind everybody of the obvious: The Morrill Act was passed during the Civil War. I think we can do this.

I will close by saying I think it's important for groups like this to remember that social support for a market economy is not given; it is earned. My business school, like all top business schools, takes students around the world for project and learning opportunities and to do hands-on things. As a dean, I have led a trip for three years to Youngstown, Ohio, and have done it deliberately to induce students away from the white-wine-and-shrimp-toast events of their other trips and toward meeting people in the heartland. I heartily recommend that journey to other schools—and to professors and policymakers.

SUMMERS: [Next is] Jonathan Macey, who has thought very profoundly over many years about our laws, particularly as they affect corporate institutions.

JONATHAN MACEY, *Professor of Corporate Law, Corporate Finance, and Securities Law, Yale Law School*: I want to explore why I find the conversations that we're having collectively about income inequality more and more these days, including in this conference, so disturbingly incomplete and unsatisfying. One is this proclivity, this urge—and I can barely resist it myself—to cite lots of statistics about rising wealth distribution and inequality. Certainly, I have plenty of statistics of my own that I could add. But I feel as though they don't really capture the problem particularly well or as fully as they might.

Like Gene, I have this notion that something very profound is about to occur. Ray Dalio, the founder of [investment management firm] Bridgewater, has captured this well. He says capitalism is producing self-reinforcing spirals up for the haves and downs for the have-nots. This is creating widening income/wealth opportunity gaps, and here's the key takeaway that poses existential threats to the United States: What Ray Dalio is saying is that there is a tremendous decline in respect for, or allegiance to, the notion that capitalism is the best system for allocating resources in society. I saw that Amherst College recently has a new guide to common shared language, in which capitalism is defined as "an economic and political system in which a country's trade and industry are controlled by private owners for profit, rather than the state. This system leads to exploitative labor practices that affect marginalized groups disproportionately." Thus we have a decline in faith in capitalism and also, concomitantly, a large increase in support for socialism.

In addition to the decline in support for capitalism and the rise in support for socialism, something that has recently been noted in the legal academy—something that is quite profound more broadly in society—is a great decline in the traditional veneration of the United States Constitution. Both on the left and the right, there's a notion that the Constitution is some kind of almost religious foundational document that people are very much running away from—this idea that we should, for example, get rid of birthright citizenship. These factors create challenges.

Of course, the next question is, what should we do about it? We are hearing all this stuff about the earned income tax credit, the guaranteed minimum income, and early childhood development education and other social programs. I'm not opposed to any of these. To me, however, what's interesting is not which particular policy proposal or proposals we should follow, but particularly with respect to national health insurance—how could it be that decades have gone by, and we haven't done any of it?

I want to turn to my views on this issue of why so little has been done. At one level, we have to face up to the fact that it's just a matter of political economy. The reason that we haven't done this is because we've not created a system that has sufficiently incentivized politicians to do anything about it. Specifically, politicians do not internalize the costs of generating unfair and uneven economic outcomes. We haven't properly incentivized politicians to do the right thing with respect to economic policy, and there are three kinds of basic problems in the political science and economic literature [that indicate] why this is the case.

One is we have a poor educational system. We have a polity that is poorly educated and uninformed, and we don't do much of anything about these problems because the polity is polarized. A recent World Bank study pointed out something extremely profound: They asked, "Under what conditions will politicians internalize the causative of poor economic performance and polarization?" This was not just in the United States; they looked at India, Pakistan, Western Europe—at many, many other countries. A key finding is that uninformed voters and polarized voters are less able to hold politicians accountable for their performance in office.

There is compelling evidence to show that the provision of public goods, and I would include national health insurance and education in this category, suffers under conditions where voters are uninformed and polarized, because politicians in polarized societies rarely internalize the society-wide costs and benefits of their decisions. Politicians are trying to benefit increasingly narrow segments of the population rather than a very broad group.

The power of the [late economist] Mancur Olson's old observation—that politicians will pursue a strategy of providing benefits to well-organized, concentrated groups and imposing costs on groups that are disorganized and diffuse—has become massively weaponized. This observation is consistent with Bob Shiller's point about how things were much better during wartime. We need something like a war or like a constitutional moment to create a sense of shared crisis that will prompt people to embrace policies that serve the good of the entire community rather than polarized special-interest groups. We need to develop a sense of being all in this together. And that's what we need to think about how to achieve.

SUMMERS: Thank you. Gene invited me to speak last and encouraged me to be as provocative as possible. Let me make a number of observations.

First, we're sitting in as elite an academic institution as exists, the Yale Law School. We need to be clear that we are a major part of the problem and zero part of the solution. I am proud of what I did when I was president of Harvard—to say that anybody who got into Harvard with $65,000 income or below could come for free. That was significantly emulated. It was a good thing to have done. It was a small step.

The second observation I would make is that if you remember one fact out of this conference, I would humbly suggest you remember this one: White people without college degrees gave 28 percent of their vote to Hillary Clinton and 64 percent to Donald Trump. While the numbers are more complicated, [statistician] Nate Silver says that exactly that pattern also characterized the 2018 congressional election. If you ask those people who they like less, business leaders or Ivy League experts—they hate Ivy League experts more than they hate wealthy business leaders.

We are not a solution; we have had complicated programs of this kind for decades. They—the people whom we identify as the central object of our concern—choose the people we regard as most dangerous and dema-gogic. [And they choose them at] 3 to 1, or 2 ½ to 1, over us. They dislike us, personally, more than they dislike the people we want to go after in their names. If we don't engage with that, we are frankly wasting our time around these topics. And I have to say that I heard a great deal here that was kind of worthy in some abstract economic sense, but I don't think was engaged in a meaningful way with that.

What are some things that I think are important and constructive, and have maybe gotten less emphasis here than they should?

First, very strong macroeconomic policies for full employment—the difference between an unemployment rate in America of 3.7 percent and an unemployment rate of 5 percent—as a social program, is larger than any social program, tax cut, or redistributionable measure that has been proposed here. That requires not elevating fiscal virtue to the top level. That requires not treating an increase in inflation above 2 percent as some kind of scandal. That requires being prepared to engage with a central macroeconomic problem for the industrialized world: underconsumption and oversaving and failure to absorb investment. [It requires] replacing the new Keynesian economics with the old Keynesian economics.

Second, we need a much sharper distinction—although it's not what most people in this room believe, and it's not really what I believe or feel— between the interests of the poor and the interests of the middle class. For people whose anger we are identifying as a center of sorrow, they'll comment about this particular focus group and think that the excessive provision of benefits to poor people is at least as large a problem as the excessive provision of tax breaks to wealthy people. Every Democratic economist thinks that it is offensive when you propose that for people who don't pay any taxes, when you invent a tax credit, you send them money. When that is called an expenditure program by the Congressional Budget Office, every Democratic economist in the world is deeply offended. They are wrong. It is an expensive program—reasonably understood, maybe a good idea. But it is not a tax cut, in the concept of a tax cut, as a reasonable person would understand it, to send a refund, to send a check, to a person who didn't pay any taxes. That we consistently claim otherwise contributes to our problems.

We need to think much harder than we do about the poor versus the middle class—about universal programs versus programs full of people who are the objects of our greater concern. If we don't, the technocratic idea that we focus everything as effectively as possible on the poorest people is part of what brought us to the political outcome that I described.

Third—and some of this was implicit in what Daniel [Markovits] and a number of other people said—the local finance of education is inimitable to fairness and equal opportunity. My old public finance teacher, [economist] Richard Musgrave, taught me that to understand issues around federalism, you basically needed to know only one thing: The rich want to live with the rich, and the poor want to live with the rich.

There is a basic competition of that kind. It is outrageous that you can live in Scarsdale, New York, and pay seventy basis points on the value of your house and have ninety-three different varieties of advanced calculus taught at your high school—and you can live somewhere nine miles away and pay 130 percent of the value of your house, and they can't afford to have any calculus taught in your high school. As long as that's true, it's going to be hard for any of this to feel fair.

The same thing is true with respect to community college, which, because it's a state responsibility, reinforces exactly these kinds of tendencies. There is plenty to be done that would make the system more progressive where you don't have to frame it as class warfare, where you don't have to claim it as tearing down the rich.

Here are a couple of examples. How can it possibly be right that if you're a $30,000 EITC recipient, you're more likely to be audited than if you're a billionaire? How can it possibly be other than outrageous that we cut the audit rate on people with incomes over $1 million by a factor of three, when the IRS estimates, without taking any account of the deterrence effects, that one more person-hour spent auditing millionaires yields $4,500 in extra tax collected?

What conceivable justification is there for the fact that maybe we should cut capital gains to a lower rate, maybe we should tax them at the same rate, whatever? What conceivable justification is there for the fact that if you're lucky enough to earn a capital gain, and you've passed the capital gain asset on to your child, there is then no tax ever collected on that capital gain? All these people who are wildly enthused about the great virtues of American capital markets and allocating resources to the best use—that is one kind of lock-in, one kind of encouragement to stick with the existing asset, that somehow never gets expressed.

There's a longer list. You can raise $3 trillion a year [in taxes], all of which will come from people with an income above $1 million dollars, when it's traced, doing things that would be good ideas to do. And that's the way we should be talking about taxes—not as a redistributional thing, not as a class warfare thing, but just as an elemental fairness thing.

Here are a couple of other examples.

Labor power—we really should be a place where it's a remotely fair playing field if you try to organize a union—and there, I'm happy to hear about and support anti-union abuse. But the idea [is] that if you try to organize a union, and your employer fires you, what you get to do is sue. If you win after five years, what you get is five years' wages. Only you don't actually get five years' wages, because if you went and got another job, you get the difference between the five years' wages and what you could otherwise have gotten. It is hard to imagine a greater set of incentives to discriminate against and fire people for union-organizing efforts than that.

We pay $0.75 a gallon for the American Society of Civil Engineers. I don't know if they really know or not, but that's what they say—that the extra payments made by Americans to fix their cars because of potholes in roads are the equivalent of a $0.75 gasoline tax.

We have an air traffic control system in the United States that has nothing to do with GPS—no role at all for GPS in the air traffic control system of the United States.

Construction is a job you do with your hands that employs people who aren't college graduates and who are left behind.

Our net investment rate in infrastructure rounded to the nearest integer over the last three years has been zero.

Depreciation has equaled the level of gross investment.

Finally—and several people have commented on it—I think the case for place-based policy is very strong. I think the case that one element of those place-based policies should be demand-side subsidies to the hiring of labor [is strong]. These are complements to the EITC that operate on the labor side.

If you only remember one thing I said, [make it this]: The way we are advocating for these policies is a complete and utter failure. Their intended beneficiaries hate us, and they hate political figures that we support. We need to reframe our advocacy.

I've tried to use examples by talking about policies that would have the desired effects in ways that are arguments for the general good rather than suggestions of anthropological compassion. I have been to too many conferences that are concerned about inequality; I think if you imagine the intended beneficiaries listening, they experience the conversation as anthropological compassion rather than as respect and being drawn into a shared enterprise.

I think that is very much related to Bob Shiller's comment about World War II. While it gives me no pleasure to say it, I think there is certainly scope for demagoguery with this strategy, so that it sedates the magnitude of the challenge posed to both our democratic ideals and our economic success and position in the world. It offers the potential for speaking about an American renewal agenda in a way that's unified.

ANIKA SINGH LEMAR, *Clinical Associate Professor of Law, Yale University*: You're right. We're not all in the same boat. I mean, to everybody's points, we all occupy very different boats. One thing I think a lot about is the way we might better occupy the same boat—the way we can address problems of segregation along racial and income lines head-on, so that we're better incentivized to invest in the resources that build up opportunity for everybody.

You're right—we're in a very elite institution that could do a better job. Why isn't at least part of the solution that places like Yale start taking everybody in as transfer students in their junior year from community colleges? We could have no freshmen and sophomores, but double the number of juniors and seniors, and double the number of our graduates?

We can think a little bit more creatively about channeling everybody into institutions in what I would suggest is egalitarianism in service of meritocracy. It is meritocratic because you're forced to rise in an institution that includes everybody, where you're not simply measured on your squash ability or your ability to excel at Exeter. The only real measure of merit is what you've done with what you've been given. Our current measure of merit isn't meritocratic at all.

JACOB HACKER, *Professor of Political Science, Yale University*: I'm surprised that nobody has talked at all about the growing interest in antitrust and addressing concentrations of economic power. Larry, I think you're right that we have to think seriously about what policies are going to appeal to the broader cross section of Americans. Antitrust is not a trivial part of growing regional inequality. It just might be something that is politically tractable in a way that some of the other ideas on the table aren't. It's kind of the opposite of the weakening of labor power. I'm not fully convinced, but this research on labor market monopsony does suggest that there are some significant effects of economic concentration. Not just on rents at the top but also on wages at the bottom.

DAVID NEWVILLE, *VP for Policy and Research, Prosperity Now*: I want to follow up on some of the comments related to taxes by a number of the panelists, which are very intriguing. One thing that struck me is what was going on in D.C. this week around a bipartisan IRS reform bill being put out in the House and the Senate about improving the tax filing system. If you think about resentments among Americans for government in general, there's hardly a bigger example than the tax system right now—the amount of complexity in this system, the steps that haven't been taken despite calls by the past Congress and administration around putting taxes on a postcard and reducing that complexity. There is obviously a lot that could be done.

SUMMERS: That's just wrong. Respectfully, for regular people, the tax system isn't that complicated. They have somebody else do their taxes. It's a problem for the kind of people who [see *complexity* as] this code word for a sense that there's a bunch of unfairness. But it's virtually a complete red herring.

NEWVILLE: Yes, for higher-income tax earners—I can't speak to that. We work a lot with lower-income tax filers, and like the earned income tax credit, that is one of the big rubs for folks. Most of them are going to get it prepared by someone else, but a lot of the problem right now is they're paying tax preparers, many of which are not regulated in any form. The IRS attempted to do this, to build in some competency standards. A lot of these returns, when they're filed, are leading to what's been called a fraud issue—the overpayment issue around the EITC. The EITC forms, even though most of these folks aren't doing the forms themselves—they're two or three times the number of pages of paperwork to claim the EITC alone than for the Alternative Minimum Tax (AMT). That's incredible, when you think about that. The AMT, which is very niche compared to the EITC, is less paperwork.

Average folks aren't doing that. They're going to something like the Volunteer Income Tax Assistance (VITA) program and having a volunteer fill it out. Or the chains—H&R Block and so forth—they have trained and competent folks. Over 50 percent of the other people are going to mom-and-pop shops. And in many states—coming back to the regulation issue—you have more requirements and licensing standards for someone cutting your hair than you do for someone to do your taxes. It's insane, when you think about it. These folks do the taxes; they send it in. When the IRS comes back with the correspondence audit, the consumer doesn't know how to deal with it. The IRS is highly underfunded, so they are doing more of these correspondence audits. The low-income consumer, working multiple jobs, is stuck on the phone line trying to deal with this. Are there some folks who fudge the numbers and so forth? Of course, but if you simplified the tax filing process, you could invest in more of those programs we're talking about that add to ROI.

Just this past week as well, Senators Sherrod Brown [of Ohio] and Michael Bennet [of Colorado] introduced a bill to expand the EITC and the Child Tax Credit (CTC). These are very bipartisan ideas. We're seeing increased research on the long-term benefits to children from the EITC and the CTC or a child allowance of some type—long-term returns to wages, to well-being, to health factors, multiple factors. This would be a great vehicle for that.

A more partisan idea is doing something like Senator Cory Booker's baby bonds proposal. Simply going back, looking at the estate tax, taking it back to what it was in 2009—that amount of money would allow for massive investments. Even to avoid the trade-off in the class warfare argument, you could say this is a trust fund for lower-income children. It applies to all children; it's targeted universalism. The lowest-income children, children of color, would get a disproportionate share, but everybody would be included, at least at a base level.

As a person who has done volunteer work with low-income tax filers, [I see that] most folks don't know when they get the EITC, when they get these benefit programs—especially all the tax benefits that came with the stimulus bill. They had no idea where that was coming from or who was giving that to them. In retail politics, we always see someone putting their name on the bridge and selling the benefits. You don't really see that at the federal level, except the Bush tax cuts, when everybody got a specific check in the mail. That is very powerful.

When thinking about trying to simplify the tax system, [why not] invest the benefits where you get the most ROI that helps the lowest-income families the most, but go further up the scale—and make sure people know they're benefiting from it? Why not say, "The government is doing this for you, and you're getting this not as a handout but because you worked for investments in your children, investments in your future, the same that the rich have"? If you do this right, you can bring down the high-end inequality and raise up the low-end inequality, and really make a meaningful difference just through the tax code alone.

OREN CASS, *Senior Fellow, Manhattan Institute*: Not to sound like a broken record on the polarization point, but especially for groups that want to assert they have commonsense answers that everyone would agree to, it would be important to have a broader cross section of the people in the room whom you need to get agreement from. One important example: Universal childcare and generous pre-K programs are not politically popular, particularly right of center, because they are considered opposed to, if not downright offensive to, the idea that women should stay home and raise their own kids. Frankly, that's something that an awful lot of families want, too. More broadly, the defect in this discussion—and in a lot of these discussions—is that they're essentially seeking ways to take exactly the model of the world that we are very happy with and finding a way to shape everybody being left behind to fit into that world, with no actual sacrifices from the side that we are happy with.

It would be terrific if more people could come to Yale. But we're talking about a population that doesn't even complete community college, which is still the majority of young Americans. It would be terrific if the low-income school offered calculus, but the fact they don't have calculus isn't the problem, if we really want to talk about what's going on in secondary school.

The reality is that for most folks we're talking about, what we really need is not something that's going to get them into a great college. It is a non-college pathway that starts in high school that's going to get them connected to the labor force with usable skills. This means either we're going to have to make all our high schools that way, and you send your own kids to extracurricular college-prep classes, or we're going to have to accept tracking. Those are the ways to do it, and that's what we have to grapple with.

It's extraordinary that neither trade nor immigration was mentioned in the entire hour of presentations. We could scream about immigration for the next seven hours, but we won't. I don't think there is much dispute that on trade, the current trading relationship with China does not bene-fit the class of workers we're talking about. That's certainly something we should grapple with.

When we ask why we're not investing more in infrastructure, when the results could be fantastic, that should come with a discussion of some-thing like the National Environmental Policy Act. How many endangered species should we be willing to wipe off the face of the earth because it's going to mean we can do a lot more infrastructure investment a lot faster? That's exactly the kind of trade-off we should be grappling with—a rich discussion that focuses not on how we cut off that top quarter of a percent, or how we feel better about getting a few more people up into that group, but how we build a society that [works] for the majority of people who are not going to achieve and don't even want to achieve the vision that we're describing. How are we going to make it work for them?

DARYL BYRD, *President and CEO, IberiaBank Corporation*: Daniel, I found your work to be interesting and accurate—disturbingly accurate. Did you do much work on this? Did you do much work relative to, say, the top half of a percent relative to the changing nature of the jobs and, say, the mobility of the jobs? If I look at inequality, checking some of the numbers, you have four to five times the national average inequality in New York City. I don't see a lot of manufacturing facilities. I'm wondering, what do those people do?

MARKOVITS: Finance and elite management are probably the two dominant things. Jacob [Hacker] showed that, surprisingly, lawyers are becoming more and more important. Profits per partner at elite law firms have gone from less than five times a secretary's salary in the 1960s to over forty times as much today. Specialist medical doctors also matter. A cardiologist was paid maybe four times what a nurse was paid in 1960. Today, a cardiologist is paid over seven times what a nurse is paid. The transformation is most extraordinary in finance. In 1969, David Rocke-feller was paid about fifty times a typical bank teller's income for running Chase Manhattan Bank. Today, Jamie Dimon makes over a thousand times a typical teller's salary for running JPMorgan Chase.

BYRD: How about the mobility of those people? Do they ever leave New York?

MARKOVITS: So, 75 percent of Harvard, Princeton, and Yale gradu-ates live in zip codes in the top 20 percent by income and education; half live in zip codes in the top 5 percent; and a quarter live in zip codes in the top 1 percent. Certainly, those zip codes are surrounded almost exclusively by other elite zip codes. It used to be the case, in 1960, that college gradu-ates were distributed evenly across cities and evenly between the cities and the countryside. It's simply not true today.

ISABEL SAWHILL, *Senior Fellow, Brookings Institution*: I want to put one new idea on the table. I also want to respond to what you said, Larry, about needing to advocate for a lot of these policies in a very different way. When I did my focus groups, what I heard was similar to what you said. I wrote my book before I did the focus groups, and I wish I'd done it the other way around. Maybe it would've changed the book in some ways.

I'll give you one example that you might appreciate. I had this pro-posal for a worker tax credit—an individual earned credit that would go up that wage scale to, say, $40,000 a year. I had a way to pay for it that I thought was pretty good, and that would work as an offset to payroll taxes. Your take-home pay would be your gross pay for a lot of people at the bot-tom. You would still have a contributory system for social insurance, but the credit would offset your payroll taxes—not replace them. But when we did the first focus group, we described it in a way that was too wonky. They didn't get it, and they didn't like it at all. I said to the moderator,

"Just tell them it's going to offset their payroll taxes and boost their take-home pay"—because that, in fact, is what it would do. For those of you who are in the financial sector, it would also be easy to administer, because it's just a negative payroll tax.

Once we changed the way we talked about it, they loved it—which is just an example of how messages do matter. When I think about these messages, I have found that if you could talk about values—overarching values like the importance of family, the importance of work, the importance of education—those three things resonate with people. There's nobody who disagrees with those three values. I am able to tell people, because of some research I've done in the past, that if you just do three things: at least graduate from high school, work full-time, and wait until you're in a stable, mature relationship before you have children. If you just do those three things, your chances of being poor will be 2 percent. Your chances of being middle class or better will be more than 70 percent.

When Mitt Romney was running for president, he used that research. I discovered in reading the ethnographic literature about this, that when he talked about this (we call it "the success sequence"), it resonated strongly with people. It's not talking about programs; it's not talking about "This is what my agenda looks like." It's really going back to basic values.

Also, I think we need to put more emphasis on pre-distribution—on what the business community can do—and less on taxes and transfers. If you give a tax credit to corporations to do more training, people would be fine with that. Business is more respected than government, and small business more than large. But big, new government programs will not cut it.

The earlier conversation we had about work and the fact that people want to earn their own income is important. I was very influenced by this book *Flow* by Mihaly Csikszentmihalyi, on how much people want to work. It's a marvelous book, and it's very well researched. It shows that even in some of those menial jobs, people get a sense of satisfaction from the fact that they're contributing, that they have that structure in their lives. I don't want to go too far with that, because obviously there's some horrible work out there. But if we could move in that direction, I think it would help a lot.

I want to go back to one issue we haven't talked about enough, and that's K–12 education. It's absolutely basic. I'm sure most of you know, if you look at rankings internationally, we are way down there in terms of what our students know. Daniel, you talked about the gap, and you were, I think, using sociologist Sean Reardon's work. There's a new study out from [economist] Eric Hanushek that is a little more optimistic than Reardon. Basically, the argument is that we've had fifty years of trying to improve things, including narrowing the gaps between high and low socioeconomic groups, and we've gotten nowhere. I was at an earlier meeting this week where we had a big discussion about it, and everybody—left, right, and middle—agreed that the problem was the teacher corps. We don't pay teachers enough, nor have we professionalized the occupation so that your pay depends on your performance instead of on a lock-step seniority system.

If we can't improve the K–12 education system in this country, we're going nowhere. But Larry is right, that the way we finance it is also a big problem.

LUDWIG: I wanted to ask a couple of questions of Larry, and it goes to the great comments that Glenn [Hubbard] and Sarah [Bloom Raskin] made. First, let's forget about 2 percent inflation. Let's put the pedal to the floor. The more people who are employed, the better off we are. In this regard, what about infrastructure spending? Would you be comfortable having trillion-dollar infrastructure legislation, irrespective of what it does to debt? That's one question.

Second, when Larry talked about "place-based policy," I didn't entirely understand. What he said was profoundly moving, about how Scarsdale gets additional benefits and inner-city New York gets fewer benefits. To Glenn's and Sarah's comments about community college and early childhood education and the importance of these, wouldn't you want to do that on a national basis so you don't have geographical bias of the kind you mentioned vis-à-vis the two different communities?

JAY SHAMBAUGH, *Director, The Hamilton Project, and Senior Fellow, Brookings Institution*: I want to emphasize one thing Larry said, because not a lot of us have talked about macro policy here. When we talk about full employment, I think the instinct people have is that it's about jobs. But it's also about income inequality, because in the top income— the top decile of the income distribution—their wage growth is almost entirely unresponsive to the unemployment rate. In the bottom 20 percent, it's massively responsive to the unemployment rate. And so staying close to full employment is usually important. This goes to something asked in the first session: Is our economy resilient?

One thing we know is that the Federal Reserve will not cut interest rates as much as it did in the last three recessions, because there is no way they will have five points of room to cut. With that in mind, unless we all think that Congress is chomping at the bit to pass a huge discretionary fiscal policy in response to a recession, I think we should be thinking a lot harder about building more automatic stabilizers into fiscal policy to make sure that we're doing more to stay closer to full employment, because it is such a huge part of wage distribution.

MARKOVITS: One thing that's important to understand is the scale of the concentration of elite education. The fact that relatively few people go through it shouldn't disguise its broader structural importance, particularly when the people who go through it have such a large share of national income. If I remember rightly, Thomas Piketty has data that suggests these institutions collectively have wealth relative to the broader society that resembles the relative wealth of the Catholic Church in the high Middle Ages in Europe. If you want a more shocking thought: If you take the ten largest university endowments and extend their growth forward at the rate that they have been growing over the past thirty years, and you take US household wealth and extend its growth forward at the rate it's been growing in the past thirty years, sometime around the twenty-second century, the ten universities will own the entire country. Now, that's obviously not going to happen. The question is, how will it not happen?

Second point: We tend to think of innovation—and especially technological innovation, particularly as it interferes with the labor market—as following its own exogenous logic. But it's not exogenous at all. In fact, innovation is endogenous to education and training. The types of innovations that have created modern finance, that have created modern management, are all innovations that would not exist if elite universities, law schools, and business schools failed to train people to deploy those technologies in the ways in which they do. That goes a little bit, Jacob, to your point: Obviously, there's a lot of rent seeking. But most of the rise of top incomes is not from rent seeking; it's from structural reallocations of labor tasks to make these people extremely productive.

On the question of sympathy or respect for the middle class, one thing that those ideas show is that the Trumpist critics of the elite—they're not wrong, not just morally but descriptively. When they say that the professional elite is something they're hostile to, it is the case that these institutions and the people they train and the way in which they restructure work and production are the cause of the immiseration of the middle class. One way to respect people is to say, "Your diagnosis is basically accurate," and then to figure out how to deploy certain forms of expertise to come up with better solutions—to acknowledge that the basic question is one in which they have been right. And if one has to be tribal, we as a group have been more wrong.

SUMMERS: I agree with much of what Oren [Cass] said—which, I think, was in the spirit of what I said. I particularly agree on doing something within schools that is less oriented to the elites. I could have added more antitrust to my list. I don't think the level of rhetoric there has exceeded the level of serious analysis. In any feasible antitrust program—define it as four times what the most aggressive Democratic administration has done in the last forty or fifty years—you're not going to move the income distribution. I think that's selling something that is the problem.

Belle's points about making all of this more attractive to the intended audience—I'm sympathetic to that. I thought I was pretty far out there on being critical of elite experts at elite institutions. Daniel has gotten flanked.

I did a lot of good in modern finance. I'm not prepared to say that somehow the fact that universities incubated modern finance means they've been massive perpetuators of privilege, and that's been a bad thing. That seems to be going a little far.

I get nervous when people get too enthusiastic about being in touch with people's values. They lose touch with what economists are good at, which is analysis about what the actual effects of things will be and whether they'll actually work out to be positive in their implications.

Gene, to your question: Right now, what we have is the rich places do vastly more than the poor places on a variety of these things. [The question is] whether I'd be for doing it nationally, uniformly everywhere, which would be an improvement, or whether I would go even further and do it nationally in the half of places that were most left behind. The proposal that [economist] Edward Glaeser and I made was for demand-side wage subsidies that would exist everywhere. The more depressed the place was, the bigger the wage subsidy would be. I think that's probably where I'd be.

If we hadn't had the Trump tax cut, and if we didn't have quite the budget projection we have, I would have been for the trillion-dollar infrastructure, debt financed. Starting where we are now, I would probably be for the trillion-dollar infrastructure partially debt financed and partially some kind of green finance, with the ability next time the recession comes to take the financing off and have it converted into pure fiscal stimulus. If the only way I could get the infrastructure was to debt finance it, I would probably be relatively tolerant of that.

Keynote Address

*Deval Patrick, Managing Director, Bain Capital,
and Former Governor of Massachusetts*

My being here, at least in my role today, may have been oversold. The notion that I might keynote at a gathering of such extraordinary thinking was ridiculous when it was first proposed. As a result, I did not write anything. I thought, *We'll have some conversation, just keep that conversation going, and it will really give me a chance to tell this.* It feels a little bit like when I campaigned for governor, the first time, in Cambridge. I know it's a poor substitute for New Haven. But you go on visits to Cambridge and someone would ask a question during the Q&A, and it was a while before I realized they had already written a book on the subject.

I'm going to make a couple of comments. I'm going to set the stage, building on some of the conversation we had this morning, and then just stop and maybe get some conversation going. I think in addition to being the wiser course, it will probably be more interesting.

I want to talk about our economic growth strategy in Massachusetts when I was in office. I want to explain why we pursued that particular strategy, what some of the results were, and what the lessons from that experience revealed or confirmed about some of the opportunities and constraints of political leadership in the context of economics.

First, I want to give some personal context. I grew up on the South Side of Chicago in the '50s and '60s, and I lived there with my grandparents in their two-bedroom tenement. My mother's sister and I were in one bedroom, and my grandparents and mother and various other relatives had a set of bunk beds. You'd go from the top bunk, to the bottom bunk, to the floor, with every third night on the floor. I went to big, broken, overcrowded, under-resourced, sometimes violent public schools. A lot of the time, my biography when I'm introduced seems to make it sound like my life began at fourteen when I got a scholarship through A Better Chance to go to Milton Academy. This doesn't do honor to the incredible teachers I had in those big, overcrowded, under-resourced schools on the South Side of Chicago, the most meaningful of whom I kept up a relationship with throughout their lives—and there are a couple whom I'd love to tell you about another time.

For all the things we didn't have in those days, we had a very strong sense of community, because that was a time when every child was under the jurisdiction of every single adult on the block. If you messed up down the street, in front of Miss Jones, she'd go upside your head as if you were hers, and then she'd call home. Right, you get it two times. And I think what those adults were trying to get across to us was that membership in community is the understanding that you have a stake in your neighbors' dreams and struggles as well as your own.

I think one of the most challenging issues that faces us today, as a national community, is whether we have any sense of that at all—whether we've been encouraged. This is why I was so interested in the whole question of national service. We don't understand or care about the stake we have in each other anymore.

When I ran for governor in 2006, I had never run for any public office. Judge [Stephen] Reinhardt was not the only one saying what an absurd idea it was. Most of my career, I have been working in or for businesses, usually as a top executive or closely with top executives. I observed there is a very bad habit of managing for the short term, emphasizing the next quarter's results, without considering the long-term impact on the enterprise. And I ran, in part, because I've seen that same behavior creep into the way we govern ourselves—where we govern for the next election cycle, or the next news cycle, and not for the next generation. I think we've been paying a price for that. I understand why that happens, and I understand that governing for the long term might, in some cases, risk a politician's career. I'm not convinced of that, but I know that's what conventional thinking is. The nice thing about my experience not being a career politician is that I could do the job without worrying about my career.

I should also say that I'm a capitalist. I made no secret about that when I was running. I don't remember it being quite as bad then as it is now. I describe myself as a pro-growth progressive, because I believe opportunity is central to the American Dream. Opportunity is made possible by economic expansion. I've made the point before that I think that has to mean growing the economy out to everybody and not just up to the well-connected.

I believe that business, not government, creates jobs, and that the role of government is to create an environment where business can and wants to create jobs. I'm also not a market fundamentalist, and I want to make clear that point. I do not believe the market is always or even mostly rational. I think that a Nobel laureate would affirm that—except in the sense that humans can rationalize anything. I remember the first time in EC 10, our introductory economics course at Harvard as freshmen, these concepts of markets were described to us as being always rational. And I said, "Well, then how exactly do you explain Jim Crow?"

So I don't think markets always get things just right. I think government has an important role in setting the boundaries or guardrails within which markets should operate, and I believe those guardrails and boundaries should reflect our better values. I think our better values here in the United States have been, or ought to be, about enabling people to achieve the American Dream.

I should say that I warned voters as well when I was running that I'm not a Democrat. I'm a proud Democrat, but I don't believe any one party or any one person has a corner on all the best ideas. And I told folks that I'd be open to good ideas from wherever they came, from whomever they came, and that I was willing to try to serve in a way that put me in touch with those ideas. By way of being close to the self-important, but being close to the ground, there are an awful lot of really great ideas that come from regular old people who are improvising to try to make their lives work. Being sensitive, close, and open to those insights was immensely important to me.

Even with all those qualifiers, I got elected anyway.

Shortly after I was elected, the bottom fell out of the global economy. The revenues we had anticipated began to disappear, because balancing budgets is legally required in Massachusetts—as in most states, I think. We had to make deep emergency cuts; then we had to go back and make more deep emergency cuts. The painful irony, of course, is that we were having to cut the very kinds of programs that people need much more broadly in an emergency. I remember that we had a Governor's Council of Economic Advisors made up of financial labor economists, a former Boston Fed chair, prominent business leaders, and such, and in one meeting early on in the recession, they told me, "Governor, we feel we should tell you that historically, Massachusetts has gone deeper into recession and stayed there longer than most other states."

I said, "OK, thanks."

So first, we did what we had to do: We froze hiring. We laid off thousands of workers, and we cut our deferred spending. We also worked with the public-sector unions to gain critical and significant concessions. One of the unions stepped up—that was unusual and important, and also substance that we could use in terms of sending important signals, again, that we have a stake in each other.

We took the opportunity that any crisis presents, to push through a number of reforms to the public pension plan and, for example, to combine five different transportation agencies that we have into one. These helped at the physical margins, but they also set a tone. And of course, we worked with the incoming Obama administration during the transition to fashion a stimulus bill that, though much maligned, was critical to stabilizing our own and other states' risks during this period. There are some important lessons I learned from that experience.

But none of that was going to be enough. We needed to, I believe, shape our own future rather than leave it entirely to chance in this so-called unseen end. If we were going to grow our way forward, we needed strategy. That strategy was ultimately very simple: to invest time, money, and ideas in education, in innovation, and in infrastructure. I'm proud to say that we emerged from the recession with some discipline and collaborative and relentless emphasis on that strategy—faster than most other states. I think we were either first or second.

By the time I left office, Massachusetts was first in the nation in student achievement, health care cooperation, entrepreneurial activity, energy efficiency, veteran services, and much, much more. We had responsible budgets, a twenty-five-year employment high, and the highest bond rating in our history. I will say that after almost a generation of young people and families moving out of Massachusetts, the end migration had turned around, and we were gaining population faster than most other states.

We did not get everything right. I used to joke, as a matter of fact, that in Massachusetts, everything wrong was my fault. Everything good was by accident, so all those stats I gave you—they just happened. But everything that went sideways was on me.

But I think, in fact, these results were not accidental; they were a strategy. I want to say just a word or two about why we chose this strategy and some of the insights or lessons gained, and then I'll stop.

We invested in education first and foremost, because education in Massachusetts is our calling card. There are some 300 colleges, universities, research institutions, and teaching hospitals within about an hour's drive. Boston has one of the most extraordinary concentrations of brainpower on the planet. And so we thought of an educated workforce and education itself as natural resources for us, and we invested there, I think, on the very same strategy that Texas invests in oil and gas, or Iowa invests in corn. That is who we are, and so how do we cultivate and grow that?

In 2007, we were beginning to appreciate the explosion of the knowledge economy around the world. I couldn't yet argue that we had an edge there. And what did that mean? We budgeted more money for K–12 education than at any time in our history. We kept those commitments with the support of the legislature and the stimulus bill, when we couldn't do it all on our own. We expanded early education opportunities. Somebody brought the issue up earlier regarding compelling data about the long-term impact of those investments. That is the kind of investment it is sometimes hard to make in politics, because the impact is going to come long after you're [out of] office, as in my case.

For instance, public higher education, which had been lagging for years—60 percent of those graduates remained in Massachusetts after graduating, so it's clearly about the future of our workforce. Through collaboration with the academy, teachers' unions, charter and other reform movements, business leaders, policy experts, and parents, we developed and passed an Achievement Gap Act, which was our next chapter in education reform—the first in fourteen years. It created a number of different innovations in education to try to get at a gap in which poor kids, kids who speak English as a second language, and kids with special needs had been chronically stuck. All of this helped us win a Race to the Top grant.

We reformed the community college system by requiring that these colleges take a larger role in workforce development. Adult education, getting at a middle-skills issue, is a looming challenge for the nation. And beyond that, we worked hard to encourage an atmosphere of collaboration among all educators, private and public. The students responded by delivering terrific results, and the achievement gaps finally began to budge. We have not solved that, but they finally began to.

We focused on innovations secondly, because there are certain industries that depend on the kind of concentration of brainpower that we have. Biotech, clean tech, digital technology, advanced manufacturing—this was another example. In each of these areas, we worked with the industry and other stakeholders, like municipal leaders, labor, and so on, to develop specific ways government can supplement and advance the growth in these industries.

The most prominent example of this would be the Life Sciences Initiative, which was a ten-year, $1 billion commitment to strengthen and expand our [state's] industry. We had similar initiatives in clean and alternative energy and in precision manufacturing, [which is] especially important in central Massachusetts, and others sized appropriately with the help of insights from industry and others, and sometimes with grudging but important votes from state lawmakers. The point for us was not to try to substitute for private markets or for private industry but rather to look for market gaps where a modest nudge by government could catalyze meaningful market growth. We also did things like fund the Cambridge Innovation Center and MassChallenge.

We cut or simplified half or more of the business regulations, many of which were just out of date. It wasn't about a point of view on the rightness or wrongness of regulation. Regulation, in my view, is precisely about that notion of guardrails that reflect community-wide interest and how we get more out of our economy—and more justice out of our economy. But many of those regulations were just stale, and so we were working with many voices, not just the regulated industries, to try to get a system that was simpler and that regulated at the speed of business. We moved much more of these services online so they were easier to navigate, and we created an ombudsperson who could take a given business by the hand and lead it through the state permit and approvals processes. We cut the business tax rate marginally and modestly, mainly because we were also eliminating many of the loopholes. So [things were] more competitive, transparent, predictable, and fair, especially to small businesses, which make up the bulk of our growth in employment in Massachusetts.

This was one of the things that was just galling. We have a corporate minimum tax; in business terms, it was trivial. I want to say it was $1,200, which is what many of our largest companies were paying as their state business tax. The small businesses were paying much, much more in many cases, so we tried to get that right. We shifted training dollars in more targeted and impactful directions. I thought this was an area in need of significant federal reform.

I made phone calls, held meetings in the governor's office, traveled around the state. I got on planes and did trade missions in different parts of the world, despite political skepticism and sometimes political heat. But I did that because my business experience taught me, having done business all over the world, that in most other places, when a senior government person shows up alongside business leaders, it frequently opens a door that might otherwise be slow to open.

I tried to be a public cheerleader for job growth wherever I could, and tried to encourage business leaders to do the same. I used to joke that I grew up in the Midwest and that when you're new, everybody brings a pie. In Massachusetts, if you're new, you're the one who's expected to bring a pie.

We did not have this sense of welcome. We didn't have this sense from the business community that we were open to encouraging others to come in of all sizes, shapes, and kinds, and in different parts of our Commonwealth, not just around Boston. Frankly, employers hearing that welcome from other business leaders—rather than or in addition to government leaders—is, I think, particularly impactful.

Among the results, greater Boston has become the most important life sciences supercluster in the world. We've had explosive growth in clean and alternative energy, the second-fastest-growing sector for jobs. We have met or exceeded our own stretch goals for solar generation, for example. And precision manufacturing is making a comeback.

We invested in infrastructure, which I always describe as the unglamorous work of government, but it supports everything else. That was about roads, rails, bridges, and airports in Boston and in Worcester, and regional airports as well, but also university buildings and laboratories, broadband expansion, public and affordable housing. Even health care is infrastructure. Anything that creates jobs today—but also a platform for personal ambition and private investment. Affording it was made possible by a number of things: Interest rates were low. Effective management of the budget with reforms and clearly articulated strategy helped us earn a stronger bond rating, which also brought our interest rates down. And our debt cap was conservative and well managed.

The [2009] stimulus bill enabled us to leverage our spending in significant ways. We tried to target what was genuinely stimulative: projects that were ready or nearly so. That complemented a job growth plan, and we tried to keep in mind regional equity—a big deal in Massachusetts, which has for a long time had a Boston-centric kind of investment focus.

We tried to innovate in how we did projects. For example, we had an accelerated bridge program that replaced fourteen bridges on the central artery with Interstate 93, which goes through the city. We had fourteen weekends with hardly any disruption in traffic, which was a great triumph.

I think some of what we were trying to do and what we accomplished was as much about tone and philosophy as anything else. First of all, there was this notion that short-termism was self-defeating, that we had a generational responsibility. We needed to leave things better for those who come behind us. That is a notion every single one of us was taught by our grandparents, but we've bleached it out of the way we govern—and [in Massachusetts,] we tried to bring that back. It was fundamental to how we argued our case: invest and govern for the long term, even if we had to make hard decisions like raise taxes, which we did. We raised the sales tax.

We tried to be equitable about how we invested, not just for the sake of spreading the money around regionally but [asking], *How do we actually encourage more of the innovation economy to touch western Massachusetts and central Massachusetts?* It turns out that our economic orientation in that part of the state is more North/South than it is East/West. When you think about transportation, how do you make it easier to get to and from New

York City from western Massachusetts, for example, rather than making it simpler to get back and forth from Boston? So [it was important to have] this notion of regional equity in mind.

I think if you go to Worcester or to Springfield today, you can see some of the impact—how we think about readying people, preparing people for the economy of tomorrow. Training has historically been done—at least as I experienced it—in a system of what I call "train and pray": Money goes to the local workforce development center. A class is offered. You go in and take the class. It may or may not have any relevance at all to what jobs are available. What we tried to do more of, with "learn and earn" programs—where there was a particular set of jobs or needs coming from a new enterprise or the expansion initiative underway—was identify particular skills and make those training dollars available to help that enterprise ready a workforce for those new jobs.

The middle-skills challenge is facing us with something I hadn't fully appreciated, but now I'm all about it. There were 170,000 people looking for work at the worst of the recession in Massachusetts, and 125,000 vacancies. What the employers were telling us was, they just couldn't find the people they needed for the jobs they had, or the skills for the jobs they had—many of those so-called middle skills. There's got to be a better word, but that's a term, and I think you know what I mean: more than a high school diploma but not necessarily a college degree. Sometimes that's a certification, with some more targeted technical skill to go alongside it.

I think there were, and there remain, certain self-defeating tropes that we have to own up to. "Government is bad"—I haven't understood that since it was first uttered in words or substance in my political consciousness in 1980. Government is us; it's you and me. And in a democracy, we get the government we deserve. What we tried to do was to invite more people to take responsibility for their own civic and political life, and then drive results that were responsive to them. I always liked the way [former US representative] Barney Frank described governments: just the name we give to the things we choose to do together.

The other self-defeating trope is "trickle-down economics"—this notion that if you just do what's right for the elites, eventually you'll get to everybody else. By the way, we knew from history that this was false when we started down this path. But now we are dealing with the much more widespread impact of that. The whole notion of community, of common cause and common state, has to be an answer to that.

The last is a slogan developed by my marvelous, bright college classmate Grover Norquist when he said, "No new taxes." I've never gotten it, and I don't say that in the way you think Democrats would say it, which is any tax is good, and more of it is good. It's that taxes are the price of civilization, and sooner or later we're going to have to decide what kind of civilization we want. This notion that government is always bad if it's big or always good if it's small is the most immature notion imaginable. We should always want government to be as small and efficient and effective as the moment demands; we should always want that. We should never want unneeded resources sent to the center if they are in fact unneeded or wasteful, but we should decide: What do we want our civilization to be? And what is our common stake in that? Then, we should align our tax system, whatever it is—income and business—to address that.

If I had a magic wand, we'd start all over.

Questions from the Audience

STUDENT: I want to ask you about climate change. We all have you to thank for signing into law the Massachusetts Global Warming Solutions Act in 2008. I think Massachusetts actually became the first state in the country to implement the Intergovernmental Panel on Climate Change (IPCC) recommendations at that time to get emissions 80 percent below 1990 levels by 2050—that's what they were saying you need to do back in 2007. But of course, last fall, the IPCC said we have to do a lot more, a lot more quickly, and actually rapidly transform our economy in the next twelve years to get to zero global net emissions by 2050 to avoid a complete climate catastrophe. I was just wondering, how does that kind of new, frightening reality factor into your work now at Bain in impact investing?

GOVERNOR DEVAL PATRICK: It's such an incredibly important question, and I don't have all the answers. But I can tell you that I think for us, the Global Warming Solutions Act, the Green Jobs Act—there was a suite of four bills, and joining the Regional Greenhouse Gas Initiative (RGGI)—these things were important within the bounds of what we could do. They were worrisome to folks who thought, *Oh dear, we've got another one of them? It's going to depress economic development and investment*—particularly when, as a part of the [2006] Global Warming Solutions Act, we committed to closing and did close all the coal-generating plants. We used to giggle about our neighbors in the Berkshires who would get all upset about how they loved the idea of wind, as long as it was off the coast of Cape Cod. Around Cape Cod, they loved the idea of wind as long as it was in the hills of the Berkshires. People generally supported the objectives, but they weren't always happy about the individual initiative right [in their backyard]. But we got that done.

RGGI was basically an early form of cap and trade. My predecessor had taken us out. We came back in. You can't do global warming state by state. You have to be global. I commend the Paris accord, and President Obama's leadership in that. I love the fact that many states, businesses, and smaller jurisdictions have kept those commitments, notwithstanding the United States having withdrawn its support for the Paris accord. I think that the other benefit of RGGI was teaching about what use we could make of the proceeds of the auction, which is what we used to fund our energy-efficiency initiative. From the perspective of my own job, we did what we could, and we set an example.

But I think this is one where we need national and global leadership. The reason why it shouldn't scare us is because we created, as we say at home, a "wicked" amount of jobs from the boundary set and the incentives created from that set of legislation—one of the fastest-growing industries at home, and one of the two that helped lift us out of recession last year. I think we can do that this year.

STEVEN PEARLSTEIN, *Author and* Washington Post *Columnist*: What about Holyoke? Does it need more than muscular government response to turn it?

PATRICK: Does everyone know what is meant by Holyoke? Holyoke was once one of the richest cities in the United States and is now probably one of the poorest. I imagine it's far and away a majority-minority city at this point. It's just a vicious cycle, and it's been going on for a long time. Springfield somehow came out of it, but Holyoke didn't. So what do you do?

Holyoke is where the population center is smaller and where the solution is probably regional rather than limited to the city. I can tell you some things we did. We put a data center there that has an incubating function to it, which had investment from state and private industry. All the big universities—public and private. They've never done anything together.

We invested in the improvement of the rail line, alongside Amtrak, at the stop in Holyoke. Because frankly, everywhere the train has ever stopped, historically, has been good for the economy. What we were not able to do in Holyoke is why I made this snide comment about politics. We have to give some context for where I'm going. We have 351 cities and towns in Massachusetts, and I think we had 275 separate 9-1-1 call centers. Every city or town has its own school district and superintendent and school committee and has its own police and fire.

There are things you can do to regionalize services—[things that] create efficiencies but also free up local fiscal money and, in some cases, state fiscal money that you can better deploy. The strategy we tried to use that worked in Massachusetts was to bring the academy into the center of the innovation ecosystem.

MIT talks about how they would just throw ideas over the back fence, and those ideas would turn into companies. The question is, how do you do that if you're not MIT? In Springfield, we had some success, right? University of Massachusetts put a stake in the ground there. Holyoke was harder and—well, people tweet everything, so I don't want to get into which local colleges were harder.

For us, in an innovation economy, the leadership of the local college or university—if they're willing to collaborate—is a powerful formula. Now, having said that, I'm going to say one last thing and stop: The vocational tech school in Holyoke is on fire. I'm talking about high school students graduating with three and four job offers at $60,000 and $70,000 to start in precision manufacturing.

And the question for us there was, how do we support that ecosystem in the central-western part of the state? Does that mean the state goes in and buys all those old factory buildings and gives it away for companies that want to do precision manufacturing and supplement the wages? I don't think so. The biggest constraint on their growth was talent. So how do you take the vocational tech talent and scale that so someone who's midcareer, not just eighteen years old, has access to it?

When I talked about trying to engage the community colleges, that's a line. I have the stripes on my back to show what that took, because they didn't want to think of themselves as vo-tech schools. They wanted to think of themselves—and I get it—as a way for folks who were not ready for four-year college to get ready for four-year college. How we got that community college mandate and leadership to embrace a broader mandate was no small task.

STUDENT: Thank you so much. I know you won't, but I wanted to express that it would be great if you'd reconsider your decision [not] to run for president.

PATRICK: You need to go talk to my wife, man.

STUDENT: What would be your advice to young people who are graduating around this time who are interested in public service, and about how we might think about making ourselves useful, wherever we end up?

PATRICK: I think there are lots of ways to serve. My own career has zigged and zagged. I'm not very good at saying, "Do this today so that you can end up there later."

The first thing to do is bring service into not just what you do but who you are, how you lead—how you bring conscience to your work, wherever it is. That's first. The power of the example you set is probably something that's hard for you to realize. And frankly, it's hard for me to accept fully, but I understand it now better than I did a long time ago.

The second is, do *something*. This feels to me—this right now—feels like a time when it's all hands on deck. And so you may not be running for something, but [you can] help someone who is. I'm not talking about which side. Back to my point: We get the government we deserve. We get a lot of what we get because a whole lot of people have just checked out, and they are staying on the sidelines. There are those in politics who plan on that.

I would [advise] getting involved in something. If it's not politics, then some other form of service—some other way of getting outside your own experience and learning how other people live their lives, how they figure it out, how they see the world. And then, in the way Louis Pasteur described, learning to listen to anything without losing your temper or your self-confidence.

I leave you with that.

Third Panel

What can be done at the local level, in cities like New Haven, Connecticut, to boost the economic well-being of middle- and lower-income Americans?

A premise of the conference—discussed at great length during the first two panels—was that most low- and moderate-income Americans are hurting economically. Aggregate measures of America's economic health have obscured any true understanding of exactly what is going on in various pockets of the country. Circumstances differ from class to class, from race to race, from ethnicity to ethnicity, and from region to region (among other distinctions), and we need to know much more than we do if policymakers are going to fashion solutions to this economic distress.

Importantly, the natural conclusion to be drawn from that reality is that the primary solutions for how to reanimate the American Dream should not be taken wholly at the national level; they need to be tailored to the circumstances facing each individual community. Others may disagree—but the purpose of the third panel was to discuss what local communities could do to turn the tide, with or without help at the national level. Several scholars on the third panel argued implicitly or explicitly that policymakers and private/nonprofit-sector leaders have a range of tools at their disposal to help right the ship. Examples abounded.

Hartford mayor Luke Bronin argued that communities in America are divided into two distinct groups: those that have caught the wave of the digitalized, information-driven, education-dependent economy and those that are struggling not to be bowled over. And as others subsequently pointed out, communities from Hartford to Baltimore to Chattanooga to Greenville to Chicago to Minneapolis have tried a broad range of strategies to expand opportunity, some of which have been more impactful than others. Those efforts deserve to be studied, compared, analyzed, and then, when proven impactful, brought to scale.

By the end of the second panel, and even more so during the third, a few things appeared abundantly clear: America faces a true crisis. If economic circumstances are truly as good as some indicators suggested, broad swaths of America would not feel so utterly left behind. The American Dream has become too elusive. But none of the conference participants believed that the nation's leaders should sit back and accept the status quo. America, they agreed, has the wherewithal to address rank inequality of opportunity, if not inequality of outcomes. So even amid domestic turmoil and dispiriting economic realities, optimism should persist.

ℭℜ

GENE LUDWIG, *Founder and CEO, Promontory Financial Group*: The national aggregate economic data—GDP and unemployment—have been highly problematic, as almost everyone here today agrees. But our focus on these numbers has gotten us in trouble—not only from a national perspective but, more importantly, from a local perspective. It is the smaller cities and towns in America that are hurting most when compared to more "cosmopolitan" portions of America. And within the more prosperous cities, it's the ethnic and racial subunits that are hurting most. Looking for solutions at the micro level is essential, and that is what our third panel is all about.

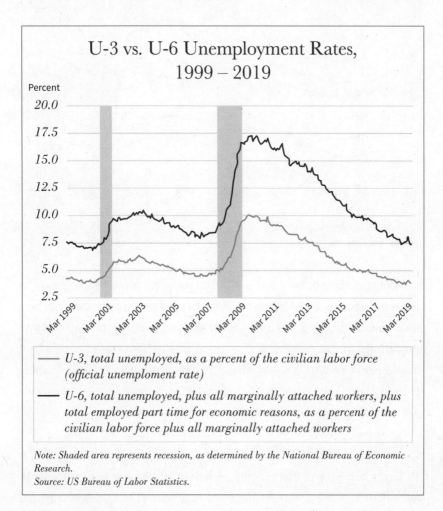

U-3 vs. U-6 Unemployment Rates, 1999 – 2019

—— U-3, total unemployed, as a percent of the civilian labor force (official unemploment rate)

— U-6, total unemployed, plus all marginally attached workers, plus total employed part time for economic reasons, as a percent of the civilian labor force plus all marginally attached workers

Note: Shaded area represents recession, as determined by the National Bureau of Economic Research.
Source: US Bureau of Labor Statistics.

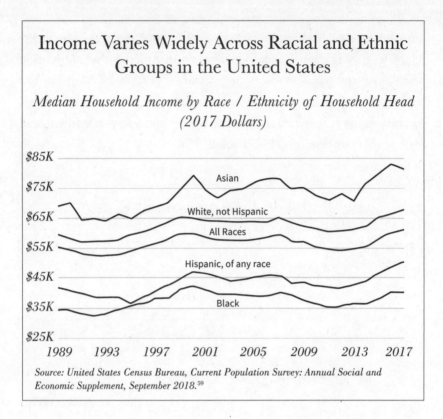

Income Varies Widely Across Racial and Ethnic Groups in the United States

Median Household Income by Race / Ethnicity of Household Head (2017 Dollars)

Source: United States Census Bureau, Current Population Survey: Annual Social and Economic Supplement, September 2018.[59]

Belle, as chair of our third panel, I'm going to turn it over to you. The question before the house is, what are the solutions that one can take on a local basis? One thing that Larry Summers said was that we have to try to even things out, from the wealthy community to poor communities. I am not sure that evening it out is what everyone here agrees to, but I am sure that everyone believes low- and moderate-income Americans on the whole need to advance economically more than has been the case.

ISABEL SAWHILL, *Senior Fellow, Brookings Institution*: This is an important subject matter, and we have a fabulous group of people to talk about it. Let me just set the stage here by trying to describe what I think the problem or challenge is.

For a long time, we had a kind of convergence that went on between different parts of the country, with poor places catching up with richer places. There was the general intellectual view that this would happen naturally from competition.

About forty or fifty years ago, that convergence began to turn into a divergence, and you saw growing inequality across geographies. Interestingly, and something that's been emphasized by another one of my colleagues at Brookings, Bill Galston, is that these growing inequalities across places also map very well—scarily well—onto some of our political divisions. That makes the case even stronger for why we need to pay attention to these place-based gaps. The conventional wisdom among economists for many years has been to invest in people and not in places. The places can take care of themselves if we take care of the people. That is beginning to change now. Larry Summers and a couple of co-authors did a quite influential paper not too long ago on the heartland, which tried to reconsider the earlier intellectual paradigm.

Jay Shambaugh, whom you'll hear from soon, has done something very similar, as have others. It's not clear what place-based policies should look like, and we have to be careful that we design them carefully. There's a lot of experimental thinking going on right now. I'm sure some of you have direct experience or other ideas about how we might approach the place-based challenge.

We also should talk about what won't work. There's the natural political pressure for governors and mayors and others to use various tax subsidies or other benefits to try to attract businesses to their community. That is nationally a zero-sum game, and probably a negative-sum game because of the opportunity costs of the resources that could otherwise be put into infrastructure, education, or other more valuable things of the sort that Governor Patrick spoke to us about: innovation, infrastructure, skills, et cetera.

LUKE BRONIN, *Mayor of Hartford, Connecticut*: I've been mayor of Hartford for three years and change. I took office in January 2016. Before that, I was the general counsel for Governor [Dannel] Malloy here in Connecticut. Prior to that, I was down at the Treasury Department for the first Obama term, first working on, among other things, post-crisis response and [the] Dodd–Frank [Wall Street Reform and Consumer Protection Act]. In the second half of the Obama administration, I was working on international illicit finance—in particular, anti-money-laundering, counterterrorism financing, and ratcheting up Iran sanctions. Prior to that, I was in the private sector for a little while and was a Navy reservist. I ran for mayor because I was frustrated with a lot of decisions I was seeing at the local level. I was a long-shot candidate, but it worked out.

When I took office, we confronted a city that was not legally bankrupt, but bankrupt. We would have had no trouble meeting the solvency test in a federal bankruptcy court. We prepared very seriously for a potential filing, and we came close. At the same time, we tried to build partnerships that would provide for another alternative.

There are some things about Connecticut, similar to what Governor Patrick talked about when describing Massachusetts, that present unique challenges when you talk about place-based strategies. [One is] this idea that you have a state of 3.5 million people and carve it into 169 municipalities—and duplicate every single service. Maybe more to the point, providing only one meaningful source of local revenue, which is property tax, results in communities where there are just enormous gaps in both need and capacity.

The Boston Fed has done some really good work on examining the need and capacity gaps. In Hartford, [that gap] is the widest of anyplace in Connecticut, and it's pretty damn wide in a lot of places in Connecticut. To put our gap in perspective: Half of our properties are nontaxable, which is an interesting and powerful statistic to cite, but it's not all that relevant. What's more relevant is, how big is the part that's taxable? The part that's taxable for us is roughly the same size as small suburbs one-fifth or one-sixth of our size around Hartford. What you get is a city where taxes are through the roof, so that the city struggles competitively and need is concentrated. Some of that is unique to Connecticut because you've got such a small geographic base, but there are plenty of things we contend with that are common everywhere.

One of those things is that regardless of the size of the jurisdiction we are talking about, we have seen such a dramatic sorting and segregation by socioeconomic status. That makes it very difficult in places where poverty is concentrated for people to figure their way out, unless there is a broader effort that extends beyond that community, beyond those borders.

That concentration of poverty is partly the result of policy failures and partly the result of conscious policy choices that continue to reinforce that concentration of poverty. I'm not just talking about policies on the national level. It's also things like exclusionary zoning at the local level and less formal barriers like an aversion to multifamily housing. Even if it's not a zoning issue, it's just awfully hard to get projects like that approved in many of the more affluent suburban communities.

As a result, it's very hard to create more economically diverse communities. Belle and I were talking about how nationally, racial segregation may be less pronounced now than it has been in the past, but that economic segregation is worse.

In Connecticut, the two map pretty well together, and our economic segregation and our racial segregation are pretty perfectly correlated. There's a lot that we can do at the national level and, potentially, at the state level to either encourage more economic diversification or discourage or prohibit those things that make it hard to achieve.

The second thing, as it matters a lot to communities like Hartford, is the criminal justice system. A few of us have been talking about trying to get the data to understand just how many individuals in any given city have been incarcerated, or more importantly, and more difficult to measure, how many families have had a family member incarcerated. It is astronomically high in communities like Hartford, and the result of that is devastating for a lot of communities for a whole bunch of reasons.

You talk about the fragility of most families' financial situation, and incarceration can be a major shock that sets the family back. It can be when somebody goes to jail and others are having to provide for their family; it becomes a major diversion of income to other family members. The trauma to family and to kids can be profound. We are a long way from correcting our mistake of the last few decades when it comes to the extent to which our criminal justice system has relied on incarceration and the inadequacy of our efforts to provide for meaningful transitions and reentry. That really is a significant driver of the inequality that we see, at least in Hartford.

I cannot overstate how many residents in neighborhoods where poverty is deeply concentrated are also wrestling and have been exposed to multiple sources of trauma. However much progress we make on basic things, like K–12 education or job pipelines or all the things that we do need to do, it's not sufficient if we don't recognize the real trauma and mental health challenges that come with living in neighborhoods where there are high concentrations of poverty and violence and addiction.

I have a lot of conversations with other mayors around the country. This is an oversimplification, but it seems to me that there are basically two types of cities in America right now. There are the cities that have caught the wave and have seen tremendous growth and have, as a result, seen tremendous displacement and pricing out of a lot of residents. Then there are the cities that essentially are aspiring to be those first cities.

The nut that we have tried to crack—and I don't know that we're doing it all that well, or that anyone's doing it all that well—is how you generate growth that is genuinely inclusive. We're trying to do that in the following ways.

First, much like Governor Patrick described, we are focusing on reengaging our business community, trying to make Hartford a hub for innovation and job growth, as it once was and as it could be, given the concentration of major employers that we have. But our major employers have, just for the last couple of decades, thought of Hartford as the place they happened to have been founded 150 years ago—not the place they're working to reinvent in and to grow. And that has changed in a dramatic way. Just yesterday, Stanley Black & Decker opened a major innovation center in Hartford. That's just the latest of about seven or eight significant steps forward like that.

Part two is, we're trying to make those neighborhood investments that give everyone in the city the feel that they are part of Hartford's rise. That [includes] taking down old, dilapidated affordable-housing projects and building new, better-quality housing in their place. We are focusing a lot on blight, and on the basics of teaching and learning in our neighborhood schools, where [education] has suffered dramatically. One of the other things that we did, which I wish we could do on a much larger scale, is experiment with something called the Youth Service Corps. That's something that we built when my administration came in, with private dollars. The theory of it was, we have a lot of kids ages sixteen to twenty-four who are disengaged and disconnected from school or from work and who don't see any real reason to go back to school, or any path to a job. We decided to create the jobs. We raised funding to create year-round, part-time employment at minimum wage: $10.10 an hour. That creates a carrot for kids to join and gives them some work experience that they can begin to put on a resume.

It also connects them to a broader network of mentorship and coaches in the way it's organized. Each core member serves on a team that's got a youth service coach who helps coordinate it. They are doing things in the community, from building park benches to shoveling snow for seniors and the disabled to creating a greater sense of investment in community and connection to community, and it works pretty well. I would love to do that on a much larger scale. We're trying to measure more effectively the success that it's had. But giving young people the opportunity to experience work—to get a work record that they can point to when they apply for jobs—and getting them connected to something that they're a part of can have a really meaningful difference.

When we look at this challenge that we face nationally, I don't think it's inappropriate for us to look back to some of the things we did during the Great Depression to create job opportunities more directly than we have been doing lately. We have about 250 kids in our Youth Service Corps. If we multiplied that by ten, we'd still have unmet needs, but I think we'd be making a pretty profound difference.

DARYL BYRD, *President and CEO, IberiaBank Corporation*: I run a fairly large regional bank in the South. We're in about thirty-three markets across twelve states, from Texas to the Florida Keys to the Carolinas— so, you might say, a southern geography.

I grew up as a fairly poor kid from South Carolina. I also had the unique experience of seeing Hurricane Katrina up close. I don't know how many people really understand it, but I can tell you, there are stories that you have no clue about. Just think about it, Luke: If you had to take everybody in your city and tell them they had to go away, and they don't get to come back for six months, and by the way, many of their homes are destroyed. It was an interesting time. It was transformational for the city.

My dear friend [National Urban League president and former New Orleans mayor] Marc Morial and I, over time, have agreed that Katrina was transformational to the city of New Orleans. But we have to respect the fact that we had an extreme loss of life in this community. We've agreed that we're not ever going to say it was good for New Orleans, because you have to respect that loss of life, which was horrible. As I was thinking about it this morning, I thought of a book I read a long time ago by Tom Wolfe, *Radical Chic & Mau-Mauing the Flak Catchers*. In the book, there are some admonitions that it may be a little dangerous for one group of people to decide what's best for another group of people, and that's maybe a little bit of a slippery slope.

We've had some conversation today that goes to that. There are lots of challenges, whether it's homelessness, inequality, poor housing, or poor education. Some of the answers—and I've seen it in my community and some other communities—seem simple. We've talked about it: it's education and jobs. I might add one more, and that's the mentor relationship for kids.

I've got another good friend, Dr. Norman Francis, who ran [Xavier University of Louisiana,] the largest Black Catholic university in the country. He's a wonderful man. He and I have talked about New Orleans and the serious crime issue we have in the city. We have a very, very diverse city—which is, by the way, wonderful—but we're trying to solve for the crime issue. Leadership in the community is trying to come together to work with the police, the state police, and the FBI to try to figure out how we get these kids to quit killing each other. They're typically young kids, and it's horrible. We're trying to get the African American ministers in New Orleans to get behind us and help us.

Dr. Francis, who is about eighty-eight years old, says, "Daryl, we just don't have the same sense of family. We do not have the same mentors for these poor kids, and they don't respect life, and it's a huge problem. We're making good progress, but education and finding jobs—it's pretty important."

[As I mentioned,] I grew up in South Carolina. We've talked a lot [today] about technical education and community colleges. South Carolina embraced technical education in the '60s, somewhat ahead of their time. Greenville, when I was a kid, was not too pretty a place. It was a textile town—or a mill town, as you'd call it in South Carolina—and they lost much of the textile business. But the community came together. You've got a couple of good universities in the area, and you had a really good technical school, and then community leadership decided that they would go out internationally and try to attract manufacturing to the city. They were successful—Michelin tires and BMW. They have some chip manufacturers in the area. But it took some vision, focus, leadership, and a thing that we seem to lack in this country today: collaboration. Because these were public-private endeavors.

Another city is Chattanooga. There's a correlation, because I lived in Lafayette, Louisiana, and we had the same experience as Chattanooga. Not all communities can have this, but Chattanooga had a public, municipally owned utility system. The utility system decided to offer fiber [optic] and broadband for the community. They actually have the fastest broadband in the country today. We did that in Lafayette as well. Chattanooga figured out that if they had that kind of technology, they could turn the community into a tech hub.

They realized [they could attract] a company like Volkswagen that was heavily into robotics to come to Chattanooga, because they could guarantee power and broadband access all the time. Chattanooga is a huge success story. Again, it's local leadership working together, because there's a big public part of this—working together, collaborating, and really turning the community around.

I'm encouraged at the local level that people still care in New Orleans. We've got a lot of collaboration. One of the things with Katrina is, it was a transformational event for the leadership of the community. Historically, people in New Orleans were probably too focused on Mardi Gras, and they just didn't focus in terms of what was really happening in the community. After Katrina, the community changed and transformed. People are very focused [now] on good government. New Orleans has become an extremely popular place. Tulane University gets about 49,000 applications for about 1,700 spots. Kids love New Orleans; we've got an influx of kids, and it's amazing. But the community has changed, and had to change a lot.

SAWHILL: Is that the local equivalent of what Bob [Shiller] was talking about earlier in terms of needing [something like] World War II?

BYRD: That would be a pretty good example.

SAWHILL: We lost a lot of life, but we also came together as a country and did some things we weren't willing to do before.

BYRD: We lost a lot of life. That's correct.

Another thing I want to discuss is a homeless shelter in Miami,

Camillus House, where they serve about 17,000 breakfasts every day, provide 17,000 showers, and house 1,100 people. Again, local collaboration is necessary to pull that off, and it makes a difference. Frankly, in New York, what happened with [former police commissioner] Bill Bratton and [former deputy police commissioner] Jack Maple around policing was amazing. They didn't get it all right—there were some things in the beginning that were not all that good—but they got it right over time. New York is a very different place than it was twenty-five or thirty years ago, from a crime perspective.

I was involved in a fundraiser a few nights ago for a new summer camp that started in the last four or five years in New Orleans. It's a camp for kids, and then they have ongoing programs during the school year. Again, it's an example of vision and leadership. We've gone out to all the different types of schools in the city—public, parochial, private—and we brought in student leaders from each of the schools. They go to camp in the summer. This is not a country club camp; this is rustic. I have a stepson who has been involved in this. These kids are developing close friends from all walks of life in our community. We have the kids in our house on a fair occasion, and it's interesting. It also gives people like me a chance to mentor to some of these kids.

But the theory is that when these kids grow up, and become real leaders in our community, they'll already have the relationships and the collaboration that'll work. It's an amazing kind of camp. They're very active during the school year as well. All these examples have strong leadership, strong vision, strong focus, in the background somewhere.

STEVEN PEARLSTEIN, *Author and* Washington Post *Columnist*: Daryl, how important were business leaders in Chattanooga?

BYRD: Incredibly important. The business community was critical to the success of [bringing fiber optics] to Lafayette as well, and we were proud to play a big lead role.

LUDWIG: How much do tax incentives matter, notwithstanding what Belle said? How much were they needed in Greenville to get this far?

BYRD: I don't remember the tax incentives in Greenville, and certainly you have the right-to-work side of both Chattanooga and Greenville.

PEARLSTEIN: I just want to make a point. What you did locally is what the business community could do nationally—and isn't.

BYRD: I actually believe some of us with large footprints are taking the lead on a national level.

PEARLSTEIN: Well, I'm going to push back on Professor Summers. I live in Washington, and the business community isn't doing the equivalent of what you just said, to get some important things done, at least on the national level. Some of that would involve pushing the politicians a bit harder to do the right thing. Or it might mean giving politicians the political cover to do what they want to do but feel they can't do for reasons of political expediency or party unity. I don't know what Reggie Jones said in 1960, but I can tell you that on most policy issues today of broad concern, the business leaders are missing in action today.

BRONIN: I don't know enough about the story of Greenville [to comment on that], but it's also back to this point about aggregates and how you measure success. I'd love to see what happened at that lower side of the income scale. You describe a place that's right-to-work, and in general has benefited from fairly low wages, and that's one of its competitive advantages.

Has that addressed the kinds of questions that we're talking about today? We're fortunate [in Hartford] right now, and as I said earlier, one of the main things we tried to do was reengage our business community in the project of rebuilding a city. And they really are engaging; they're doing that, but that effort isn't in tension with their other goals. Do we need our business community at this point to be comfortable advocating for some things that might be in tension with their other goals, their bottom line, and their feeling about the taxes at the top marginal income-tax rate? Those are very different asks to make of the business community.

PEARLSTEIN: Well, that's what leadership is: making short-term sacrifices for long-term gains. And we don't see that at the national level.

BRONIN: I agree. What I'm saying is, I'm sure that in a lot of places you see the business community coming together in ways that they can be powerfully helpful and that are largely cost-free. But I'm not sure that they're coming together to be powerfully helpful in ways that are costly.

MARY MILLER, *Former Under Secretary, US Treasury Department*: I'm going to talk about Baltimore. I would have to begin by saying this is not an example of what's going well right now. Maybe last month you saw the Sunday *New York Times Magazine* cover article called "The Tragedy of Baltimore."

When I left Washington to come home [to Baltimore] in 2015, one of the first things that happened was the death of a young Black man in police custody. Today, we lead the country in violent crime. We've had four police commissioners since 2015. We've also had a breakdown in political leadership in this city. Last week, the mayor took an indefinite leave of absence, and the governor began a criminal investigation into some payments she received for books she had written.

What I see locally is a real breakdown in trust in the police and government and in the financial sector. A couple of months ago, I was almost impaneled on a murder trial in Baltimore when 30 percent of the prospective jurors said they would not believe the testimony of a police officer in Baltimore. This is not a great time for my city.

We don't see great private-sector leadership today. The private sector is not happy with what they're seeing: political leadership, crime statistics, and the whole environment. Many of them just have a one-foot-out-the-door attitude, which is, *When my lease is done, I'm out.*

This is going to end on a happier note, but I wanted to set the stage for a large American city that is really struggling today.

I took a seat two years ago at Johns Hopkins in their 21st Century Cities Initiative and decided to use my financial-sector background to look at every financial flow in Baltimore to a small company or small business. I make the distinction because we were measuring venture capital investments in startups in Baltimore and loans to what I would call main street businesses in the city. Because Baltimore is both a county and a city, it was actually pretty easy to get the data at a very precise level for the city. What we saw was a pretty good story on venture capital.

We followed 250 companies that have been funded over ten years. Of that, 66 percent of them were alive and well in Baltimore; they had created 4,000 jobs and a steady progression of venture capital. That's something that we will certainly encourage.

On the bank lending side, we saw a complete collapse of bank lending in the city over ten years. From 2007 through 2016, the number of loans was down by more than 50 percent, and the dollar value of those loans was down by more than 30 percent.

At the same time, bank deposits in the city have doubled from $13 billion to $26 billion. Had these depository banks made the same number of small business loans in 2016 that they had in 2007, they would have lent $600 million as opposed to $200 million.

You can see where the gap is developing.

I will acknowledge that it is much easier to measure the supply of capital than the demand for capital, and reasonable people would say, "Well, how much demand is there for a loan in the city of Baltimore today?"

I would say there is tremendous *discouraged* demand in this city. Some of the confidential data that we've gotten from banks would suggest there is a very high decline ratio on loan applications—the ones that even make their way through the door.

To Larry Summers's point earlier, I'm not trying to romanticize small businesses. But right now, for Baltimore, organic growth is our only hope. We can't expect to attract companies to move into our city; we really need to be working at ground level.

So how did we get here? What has happened?

The trends in Baltimore are not really different from national trends, in terms of bank consolidation and some contraction in small business lending, but they are worse in Baltimore. First, we lost every large locally headquartered bank over the last decade. The large national banks that now are in the city don't want to make small, inefficient loans to small businesses.

The average size of loans has dropped significantly by more than two-thirds. The average loan today, including credit card loans, is about $37,000. We're not going to turn the clock back and get large banks to do things that are not efficient or economic for them.

The second thing we note is this city has been focused on real estate lending, secured lending, bricks and mortar, and not at all on small business lending. At every level, we've lost the art and practice of making small business loans. I know you're going to say, "Well, what about online technology?" et cetera. That is not filling the gap right now; we have more data on that.

Third, we also never really developed the capacity and the institutions—like community development financial institutions—to do small business lending, and that's part of the solution.

Finally, we've had very weak initiatives at the state and local levels to support small businesses and growth from that dimension.

So what can be done? At the federal level, one thing I'm really watching is the work to modernize the Community Reinvestment Act (CRA), a forty-year-old law, to encourage deposit-taking banks to lend back into their deposit base.

We pulled all of that data on the banks in Baltimore, and it is really shocking how old it is, how irrelevant it is—how it doesn't measure small business lending. There's a lot that could be done at the federal level to tighten that up and modernize it, to really connect banks to the areas and the places that they should be serving.

In Baltimore, our best hope right now is actually the nonprofit sector. I do not see leadership from the private sector or the political leadership right now to really strengthen the financial capacity of this city, which is really critical. We do have strong anchor institutions in our universities and our foundations, and they are very interested in helping. That may be where the dynamic goes for a while, because I don't think we will have an elected mayor again until January 2021.

I have been working to try to rebuild—or to build, rather—the capacity of community development financial institutions (CDFIs) to restart lending in the city. We have to ask our largest banks to help capitalize those CDFIs to get it done. These large institutions at the top of the house are clearly interested, but at ground level it's just not happening. We need to get to ground level to say, "We need your branch managers to work with us and funnel almost-bankable loans to our CDFIs. We need capital from the banks to help fuel lending."

We could do more at the state and local levels to really leverage the limited public dollars we have. I've identified all these little public loan programs that should be completely transformed to loan guarantees or loan loss reserves, to let the private sector do the lending and give them a backstop.

One area that we have been good at is being proactive on opportunity zones. One of the local foundations has funded an opportunity zone coordinator, who is really trying to connect capital to projects in the city. Our view is that we don't want stateless capital to just come into Baltimore, rent their tax break, and move on. We want to have investments and investors that want to see the city move forward.

The biggest elephant in the room in Baltimore is that we have to absolutely acknowledge, discuss, and move forward on the question of racism, redlining, and the historic practices that have really cemented so much of the poverty and the disinvestment in the city. We need to find a way to do that pretty quickly.

SAWHILL: I'm glad you mentioned opportunity zones; they haven't come up yet, and they are a new wrinkle in all of this. And I know that when Oren [Cass] and I were working on this report I've mentioned a couple of times, we came out in favor of them. But we made the point that these financial tax incentives by themselves aren't going to work unless they're combined with leadership and collaboration, and the other things that need to go along with that: skills, training, infrastructure, everything else.

It needs to be part of a broader plan. Do you agree with that?

MILLER: Yes, I do. I forgot to mention that the state just passed legislation this past week, requiring transparency on opportunity zone investments—because the federal law doesn't really require much information about who's investing—but also offering some more state incentives for investors that do provide the transparency. They're trying to wrap around it some better governance and better transparency about the investment.

SAWHILL: The other critique has been that the political process has selected areas that are not all that disadvantaged, maybe gentrifying around a university. Is that a problem in Baltimore, or Maryland?

MILLER: We have forty-one opportunity zones, and some of them are contiguous to areas that are really taking off and would probably attract some investment irrespective of [the opportunity zone]. It's a mixed picture. But I'd also say, for investors, there's an opportunity for real return in Baltimore, because the cost of entry is very low. That's the whole reason for having a coordinator who is staying on top of it and making sure that we don't lose control locally.

MICHAEL MOSKOW, *Vice Chair, The Chicago Council on Global Affairs, and Former President, Federal Reserve Bank of Chicago*: The message, just based on what we've heard so far in this panel—about Chattanooga, about Baltimore, about New Orleans, and what you'll hear about Chicago—is that the problems all differ. These are local problems, and they need to have local or special policy approaches to deal with them.

Just a couple of words on my background. Early in my career, I worked at the Labor Department and [the Housing and Urban Development Department]. I taught economics, and I was in business for fourteen years. At a later time, I went back into government and was deputy trade representative. Then I ended up at the Chicago Fed, where I was the president for thirteen years.

I've been very heavily involved in Chicago and the metropolitan area as well. Chicago, by the way, is about two and a half million people, and the metro area is about nine and a half million. What's unique about Chicago is the business community involvement in problems this city has and in policies for the city. That goes back to the fire in 1871, which probably was our World War II in a sense, because many parts of the city were completely destroyed.

[Back then,] the business community funded Daniel Burnham, a very famous architect, to do a report on what should be done. He wanted to help give green space to inner-city people. He recommended that the whole Chicago lakefront, twenty-one miles, be parkland. The business community said, "That's a great idea." They took it to the city, convinced the city to do it, and that's the way it is today. From a quality-of-life standpoint, that was a huge step forward.

That's the tradition—the business community and the city always work together, no matter who the mayor is, what political party, what background. It's a very close relationship with business. I'm involved with an organization called World Business Chicago, a public-private partnership to help attract business firms to locate there. The business community also puts up money for individual charter schools. It's a very, very strong relationship.

Let me say a word about employment opportunities and human capital, and about violence and gangs.

On the employment opportunities, we talked before about the business climate being important, and Gene talked about quality regulation. Ditto at the state and local level, as well as the national level. Equivalently, quality of life is a very important part of cultural activities. The financial stability of the city and the state is a serious problem. We're the worst state in the country in terms of our bond rating; we have the most debt, we have the most payables, and so forth. I know Connecticut is close, but Chicago and the state of Illinois are neck and neck as to who's going to be the worst.

We have real pension problems as well. The state has lost 35,000 people in the last year through migration. A lot of the outward migration is African Americans, interestingly, which surprises a lot of people, but it gets back to the violence—that is mostly against minorities, in minority communities.

In terms of attracting firms to the city, I was a bit surprised [about what] we've been learning lately—that with all the problems we have with financial instability and the publicity on the violence, the single most important factor in attracting firms to Chicago is the quality of the workforce. That's number one by far. The firms that are looking to locate will say, "We're aware of the problems, and we know taxes are going to go up in the future. But do you have a quality workforce?" This is something that we have focused on a great deal, and that gets to the whole human capital issue and the skills shortage we have.

Our public schools are better; they're not where we want them to be, but they are better. The charter school movement has been important in Chicago in encouraging other schools to improve. A little competition really did help here. We're never going to have everyone in charter schools. That's not the intention, but it's to encourage the other public schools—because charter schools are public schools—to improve.

Also, on the community college side, outgoing mayor [Rahm] Emanuel came up with the idea that anyone who graduates from a Chicago public school with a B average can attend community college for free—no charge whatsoever. They have a complete 100 percent scholarship. He has focused on restructuring the community colleges, too, and there has been some good progress.

On the violence and gangs issue: I talked to Mayor Bronin about this. Gangs in Chicago seem different from gangs in Hartford, but regardless the violence is, obviously, a very serious issue. Our number of murders and shootings is higher than both New York and Los Angeles combined. We've made some progress, but not nearly as much as we want.

The gangs seem to be, at least in Chicago, a substitute for family—substitute for the male not being present in the household. It just gets back to the points made before about the importance of family, education, and work. Family is a very important part of this puzzle.

In terms of the criminal justice system, we have a new mayor who will take office next month. The election turned out to be a very unusual system where there are no political parties. Anyone who wants to run, if they get enough signatures, can run. We had sixteen candidates running. In the first round, if you got 50 percent of the vote, you would be the mayor. Number one received 19 percent; number two received 17 percent. Bill Daley—brother of Rich Daly, a former mayor—came in third, and he was out. So we ended up with the top two: Lori Lightfoot, who will be mayor, and Toni Preckwinkle, who headed Cook County and the Democratic Party in the county.

It was a reformer versus the establishment, and the reformer got 75 percent of the vote, so it was overwhelming. She has a background in criminal justice. She worked for Mayer Brown, one of the top law firms in the city. Her mentor, interestingly, is a very conservative Republican, also at Mayer Brown. She praises the help that he has given her, and he praises her. It's an interesting relationship. She headed a board that reviewed some of the activities of the police department, too. She has some background in this area, and I have high hopes that she will be able to step in and make further progress on the criminal justice system and on getting the police force and community to be more in sync.

SAWHILL: Now over to Jay. I want to give a shout-out for your latest book on place-based policies, *Place-Based Policies for Shared Economic Growth*, because I certainly have found it very useful. You might want to tell people a little bit about that and your background before you dive in.

JAY SHAMBAUGH, *Director, The Hamilton Project, and Senior Fellow, Brookings Institution*: I'm the director of The Hamilton Project. For those of you who don't know it, our mantra is that we try to find evidence- and analysis-based policy proposals and try to pull academics into writing things that policymakers can digest because they're not written for a journal; they're written to actually go ahead and do. As Belle mentioned, recently we did a book on place-based policies, where we did a lot of work on regional inequality. One of the things that the work we've done over the last few years really emphasized is the number of things state and local governments can do. There's a lot.

The problems we've talked about so far today, in many cases, involve these big, structural, tectonic shifts. But there are a lot of smaller things you can do that would have meaningful impacts on people's lives.

One of the numbers that really struck us when we were looking at regional inequality—just to keep in mind how important this is to the national aggregates—is the employment-to-population rate for prime-age workers in the bottom-quintile counties; it's more than fifteen percentage points lower than it is in the top quintile. For context, in the Great Recession, the national aggregate fell five points, and we freaked out. It's as if the bottom counties are facing three great recession shocks relative to the top.

That is not very optimistic, but the optimistic thing is that there are a lot of policies that have meaningful impacts. I'll echo something we have heard today: Education—K–12 education not strictly geared toward college readiness but geared toward getting people through high school—is crucial.

The question is, what can a place like New Haven do? New Haven's high school graduation rate has been increasing, but it's 80 percent. One in five kids who hit the high school system in New Haven leave without a high school degree, which we know—just looking at any data set—tells us they will have worse employment outcomes, higher unemployment rates, lower wages, worse economic outcomes in life. There are a lot of evidence-based policies that researchers have studied about how to combat chronic absenteeism, how to use tutors, how to use text messages to parents, how to do lots of things to try to get kids at least through high school.

A lot of what we've heard about training is really important. Training doesn't always work in the United States. There are a lot of bad training programs. The one good thing about that, because they're so varied, is we can compare them and see what works. And we do know that when you get community colleges paired with the cities, paired with employers, you can come up with training systems that work.

Minnesota does some really interesting stuff where they use big data scraping to figure out what all the job postings require, and then they use that to inform the training. There's a lot that can be done there.

Also, [we can do] more on reentry into the training programs. There are too many people, when we worry about lower- and middle-income people, who are just locked out of the labor market because we don't practically move them back from prison, back into the labor force.

All the federal safety-net policies we have then turn into local issues, because so many of them are administered at the local level. We need to make sure people eligible for these programs are getting [the benefits of] them.

If you are a poor kid, having [the Supplemental Nutrition Assistance Program] (SNAP) in your household makes a huge difference to the likelihood you go through school successfully. Making sure the families that are eligible for these programs actually get them is something that states and, in particular, cities can be trying to do, and they can have a real impact on people's lives.

The one place where the different needs of different cities really shows up is in housing. For the cities that are in what Luke [Bronin] refers to as the first tier, it is really important to let housing supply expand with jobs, because there are a lot of people in communities across this country where employment rates are really low who would like to move somewhere where there are more jobs, but they're locked out. I don't think that means we try to tell everyone they've got to move, because frankly that's obnoxious and not remotely what everybody wants. But there are people who do want to move, and trying to make sure there are places they can live where there are jobs is really important.

It was funny that Zach [Liscow] talked about buses earlier. We've talked to some transportation economists about what we could do for growth, what we could do to help lower- and middle-income people. The answer was that a lot of stuff doesn't work, but poor people take buses [anyway], and our bus routes are often terribly designed, really inefficient. If you spent time trying to make sure you connect where poor people live to where jobs are, you can do a lot to improve some people's lives.

Is that a winning political campaign, or something that combats forty years of scale-biased technological change? No, but it can help some people.

At the state level, I would really emphasize that you could let the labor market be a labor market. Far too many people are bound by noncompete contracts and can't construct their own business and can't compete for new jobs and can't move up a job ladder, on the one hand. Far too many people can't get into professions because there are occupational licenses that have way too burdensome a licensing setup to get into them. We could just make it easier for lower- and middle-income people to get the jobs they want to get.

We had some place-based policies that would be better if they were funded and run at the federal level, but you could employ them at the local level, too. One example is, if you look at census tracts that have really high poverty, the biggest problem there is that there are no employers. You could pay nonprofits to hire people in those communities to fix up the public goods, which are almost always deteriorating in those communities, to give those people a set of skills. You could have them clean up parks, fix schools, work in community health centers. Pay them for a year and a half, at which point they have some skills; they're on the job ladder. Then subsidize their wages in the private sector for a little while until they're more employable, and they're off and running.

Lastly, because we're here at Yale, I would just echo what Governor Patrick talked about—partnering universities to the local employers is hugely important. Universities create a supply of highly educated workers, but that's not what's important, honestly, because they can leave. What matters is whether you have demand for high-skilled workers in your city, in your town, and trying to partner the research out of the university. Maybe tossing it over the fence works at MIT, but it doesn't work in most places that way. There are lots of programs that are takeoffs from the manufacturing-extension partnerships that really could do more to make sure universities help the local businesses have demand for high-skilled workers. New Haven does this well, actually.

It doesn't get talked about enough in economic policy circles, [but] one thing we do terribly for lower- and middle-income people is that too many communities now fund themselves off criminal justice—fines and fees. But New Haven is in the third percentile, the very bottom of funding criminal justice expenditures off fines and fees. So, good for New Haven. More places should follow that [example], because in far too many places, one mistake—and a minor one—can cost you your entire financial life.

We should do better.

ANIKA SINGH LEMAR, *Clinical Associate Professor of Law, Yale University*: I have the privilege of teaching at the Ludwig Center for Community and Economic Development. I'll talk a little bit about what we do.

Gene, earlier you referenced eyes and ears, and observing what's going on in the world. Part of what the clinic does is serve as eyes and ears. Our mission is to work directly with low- and moderate-income communities. Our mode of operation is to credit and support the implementation of initiatives that our clients in those low- and moderate-income communities have identified as things that will improve their lives and their communities.

What is it that our clients identify as needs? There is a [large] range at the outset. I should say about half of our clients are in New Haven, but we also have clients elsewhere in Connecticut. We have a couple of clients that are out of state for one reason or another; usually it's because there is something particularly innovative going on elsewhere in the world that we'd like to learn about. We will go to D.C. or upstate New York or St. Louis or wherever that thing is happening.

Among those clients, there is a [large] range in terms of what they identify as their needs when it comes to advancing economic opportunities. Their needs run the gamut—from accessing financial services (particularly small business and startup funding), to [accessing] affordable and healthy food in the neighborhoods where clients live, to confronting racial justice in the criminal justice setting and in all sorts of settings, to helping parents address childhood trauma and how to raise children in neighborhoods that can give rise to experiences of trauma, and more generally, to helping build the sort of civic infrastructure that's central to the social fabric of their community.

Behind it all, particularly in New Haven, there is the background of jobs and job loss. At the beginning of every semester, I do a bus tour with my students around New Haven. I tell them it's an imperfect but necessary way to learn about the city we live in. It takes about three hours. When we go, every neighborhood in New Haven—every single one, including what are now well-off communities—has an enormous factory building that once was home to tens of thousands of jobs. In the most significant case, 80,000 jobs were lost in what was the old Winchester Repeating Arms. That is a really important visual for them to see, that the engine of our economy during the period when the city was growing just doesn't exist anymore.

Among the whole range of things that our clients identified, three things are the biggest, most common things we work on.

One is housing. When I came to Yale six years ago, we had a number of affordable-housing clients, largely based in New Haven. One thing I've done is expand the number of nonprofits that we represent that are doing housing development outside of the city. That's acknowledging the problems—the poverty concentration, and the need to do affordable-housing development not just in our low-income neighborhoods but in other places. It might provide different types of opportunity for the people who are living there.

Housing, of course, is shorthand for a lot of different issues. It's shorthand for income problems; if your income is low, you need to lower your costs and have more affordable housing. It's shorthand for safety, trauma, school quality, the ability to accrue wealth—which is a hard one for us, because people point to housing as a mechanism for wealth accrual. Housing is a necessary pathway for wealth accrual, but at least among our clients, all the homeownership programs that we're working on, that are subsidized in various ways by the federal and state government, are not pathways to wealth. These programs are concentrated in communities where housing values are not likely to go up anytime soon. And they come with restrictions on resale, so that the focus on homeownership as the wealth-building mechanism is complicated.

Two is education, and particularly in the pre-K and the post-12 spheres. We do a lot around early childhood, both in terms of making high-quality early childhood cheaper and more accessible and in terms of building up quality. Then there is the job-training piece. We have a client who is currently working to advance existing programs in one of New Haven's larger high schools—to do certification and training programs inside of the high school, embedded in the high school experience. Rather than graduating and then taking out a loan—or forgoing, let's say, a certified nursing assistant training program, which is not [as] expensive [as college] but is still prohibitively expensive for a lot of people—you do it as an after-school program inside of the high school. You graduate with your high school and your certified medical assistant degree at the same time.

The third piece is entrepreneurship, where we're looking at access to capital, but we're also looking at the ways in which entrepreneurship is very tightly regulated. Some of the lowest-margin forms of small business are also some of the most highly regulated. Food production, childcare—these are things we're working on to decrease the regulatory burden. At the same time, we're trying to connect people to financial services that would enable them to start those businesses.

There are lots of reasons to be optimistic. There are good ideas with return on investment here. We can bring down people's housing costs. We can bring down their early childhood costs and improve quality. We can support low-income entrepreneurs in sustainable ways that reap benefits for their communities. But there are also some reasons to be pessimistic, and I'm glad Mayor Bronin prefaced some of them.

There are some basic resources that are required to build economic opportunity. They are generally public goods, and here in Connecticut—maybe more so than nationally, but also nationally—those resources are highly segregated. We don't all occupy the same boat, and for the most part, the well-off among us opt out of using, and therefore funding, those resources that create pathways to economic opportunity for the poorest people and often for middle-income people as well. In the clinic, we think about integration along race and economic lines as well.

SAWHILL: This is a rich and diverse set of perspectives we've heard. I'm imagining some of you might have questions for each other, and, Mary [Miller], you should get priority here if you want to ask any follow-up questions. I also want to bring in anyone who hasn't spoken recently.

ZACH LISCOW, *Associate Professor of Law, Yale Law School*: I'm delighted to have all this discussion on place-based policies. I want to pick up on that thread, so this is a thought on what the federal government should be doing on a place-by-place basis. In my class, which I teach here on economic and tax policy and what you should do about income inequality, we read [Larry Summers's] paper on place-based policies, ["Saving the Heartland: Place-Based Policies in Twenty-First Century America"]. Basically, it's an efficiency justification for encouraging job creation in depressed places.

Something that I've emphasized to my students is that it's important to think through why you're doing a program before you get to a solution to the program. There are many reasons why you might want to have place-based policies. One of them is efficiency: *We'll grow the economy somehow through having special place-based policies.* Another one is anti-right-wing populism. There are lots of depressed places in the country, and maybe you want to help them out so that we have a healthier body politic. I ask the students, "Depending upon which justification you have, how would you have different policy solutions?"

It turns out that one of the solutions in that paper is encouraging the presence of military bases in areas that are more depressed. Periodically, we have these closings—we have these panels that decide where to close military bases. The students say, "We want to encourage military bases in these depressed areas"—which might be good if you want to encourage jobs in these spaces. But if what really motivates place-based concern at the national level is stopping right-wing populism, one student pointed out, maybe you don't want to have military bases around in these really depressed areas, because military bases might just radicalize what is already a radicalized group of folks.

I'm not sure what many people here would think would be the right justification. An important reason for place-based policies is stopping radicalization, and [issues] along the lines of the examples I just gave would affect the types of policies that we have. In particular, we want to have policies that not only encourage employment but encourage employment in particular ways that help integrate people into the broader economy.

ANDREA LEVERE, *President, Prosperity Now*: I'm going to follow up with recommendations of practical things that are underway and ways we can connect to them.

First, [Prosperity Now is] conducting a national initiative called Building High Impact Nonprofits of Color. We are doing it in New Orleans, Baltimore, Miami, Dallas, Wilmington, and Chicago. We have a group of more than forty organizations that have been building capacity, financial resources, and policy knowledge—all of which span affordable housing, entrepreneurship, and a whole range of other things. I've already talked to Mary [Miller] about connecting her with these organizations, but it's been astonishing how siloed they are from the mainstream community development field, even if they're in this field, and how much they could benefit from added financial capacity or knowledge in their work. We're interested in making those connections.

The second piece concerns the role of CDFIs. Rather than thinking of starting a new one, I really think that helping CDFIs that exist expand into new areas to achieve those economies of scale and leverage their balance sheets [is a better solution]. The largest CDFIs now are going directly to the capital markets and raising capital.

The third piece goes to this Youth Corps initiative. [At Prosperity Now,] we've just completed a project working with five large youth employment organizations in the country that are integrating financial capability and savings into their programs. We're helping train the staff to deliver financial capability skills directly as part of their workforce training. That starts to transform things from the get-go because the youth get banked right away, and then they also profoundly change how their families build financial stability. One of the most interesting things is how many of their parents have bought homes based on the training and resources that we brought to these youth.

The last piece is the whole connection between health and wealth. Obviously, in Baltimore we know that Johns Hopkins is a primary economic driver of the city. We're working with the Robert Wood Johnson Foundation on how to leverage all balance sheets of anchor institutions on behalf of expanding economic mobility.

Particularly, it's health care institutions. If they do Medicaid work, they have reserves that could be invested in addressing the social determinants of health. Kaiser is investing $200 million into affordable-housing investment in California and elsewhere, because they understand that they need to disrupt the upstream determinants of health—how we can advance that practice, and a piece of that is engaging CDFIs.

The final strategy relates to our EITC work—specifically, an initiative called StreetCred. It was started by several pediatric residents in Boston who would send in their patients to VITA sites to get their taxes done for free and collect their refunds. But they found that with the Boston transportation system, their patients would get there too late, and the sites would be closed. So the residents said, *Let's just open a VITA site in the waiting room of the pediatricians: While we are waiting, we can get our taxes done.* This year, the Yale New Haven Hospital did the same thing. There are all sorts of ways to leverage not just the real estate. But these pediatricians are the leaders in all of this work nationally that we are doing together.

I am the chair of the Community Advisory Council for the Federal Reserve Board of Governors, but each of the [Fed] banks also has a Community Development Advisory Committee. We had a briefing session a month ago where many of the committee members told the Fed economists that the two data points presented on unemployment and inflation rates do not describe what is really happening in their communities. We should sit down with the Fed economists and see what we might be able to do to come up with exactly the metric we want. I'll need your help on that, Jacob [Hacker], to figure out what that metric is. I think they're open to this, and we already have a meeting with your entire research statistics team, to begin to look at what we might be able to do.

JACOB HACKER, *Professor of Political Science, Yale University*:
I always look forward to the business part of these conversations when we
start talking about the upper level, because then, all of a sudden, all of
these constructive ideas get to the table. One of the useful features of the
conversation so far is that now we're situating this in the larger, politically
common context. Zach [Liscow], I'm surprised that you framed it the way
you did, because don't you think backlash is a big problem for dealing
with these economic problems in the long term? Isn't it anti-efficiency
to have political backlash? If you think about it in the political economy
sense, these [issues] are not as sustained.

That's the point I want to make. Every time we start talking about
the local level, and we think about the travails and the triumphs, we often
forget about the ways in which that's situated within this larger political-
economic structure that we're talking about. I want to put on the table a
few propositions that link up a lot of what's been said about the way you
can change the role of the different levels of government—the way it's
going to facilitate what the cities are doing. Just because cities are on the
ground [doesn't mean they] have the capacity to do that.

One thing that hasn't come up is that we really have abandoned revenue sharing in the United States. That is really striking when you look
at it. The way in which local government and even state government are
structured, you're going to create profound inequalities if you don't have
some means of essentially moving revenues across places.

I throw that out there because it changes the incentives fundamentally
at the local level. We did talk about the state regulation of the labor market,
but not state preemption laws. Cities are now—especially in the South—
increasingly bound by state rules. That raises a fundamental point: We
want to have power at the right place. The resources and power don't necessarily have to be coming from the same place, and sometimes you want to
constrain people. But you don't always want to. These are bad constraints,
but there may be good ones, like constraining cities against doing excessive
incentive packages, for example, because there's an arms race.

The municipal politics that operate at the city level make it hard for cities. They need the revenues, and they also need the spur. While the states need to open up labor markets, cities aren't going to be able to deal with some of the backlash against higher-density housing without an assist from higher levels.

I don't have a set of clear prescriptions, but it's useful to think about how you might enable cities in a way that's realistic to the things they do well and the things they can't do well. What is the context in which business and other people will invest rather than smash and grab? That's the challenge that all these cities are facing.

LISCOW: I completely agree with your point [about] narrow efficiency. I mean, to put it simply, Larry, efficiency.

HEATHER GERKEN, *Dean and Sol & Lillian Goldman Professor of Law, Yale Law School*: One thing that really strikes me about that is, there are many differences among the cities and states in this regard. I do agree with Jacob—if you want to imagine where you could get solutions moving on the ground, I always think the state is an easier level than national. But what states and cities always lack are capacity and technical expertise. Everyone has to reinvent their own wheel.

I'll just give an example from my world: City lawyers and state AGs don't have the technical capacity to actually use the legal powers in their possession to the extent that they could. One of my students has created a network that's enabling them to share expertise, share knowledge. If I were investing, part of what I would invest in is that [expertise and knowledge]. I trust the mayor to be able to move the politics he needs to move [an issue]. But he's going to need an army of experts behind him that he's never going to be able to have the resources to hire. I know that's true of New Haven; I know that's true of most states, actually. Even state legislators are vastly [outgunned] compared to the work that they need to do.

As a result, they rely on lobbyists, right? The American Legislative

Exchange Council (ALEC), and all those folks. There needs to be a counterpoint to that, to provide that sort of intellectual infrastructure and technical infrastructure [states and cities need] to enable them to follow these solutions. That is something that, for whatever reason, because we're looking only at the local level, we think about putting in place in one city. But we don't think enough about how to put it in place in all cities and what that structure would look like. If I were casting my vote, I would just say technical expertise and the ability to help everyone to scale would be really useful.

LUDWIG: It seems almost insane to think that Hartford, which is relatively small and poor, is somehow going to fund everything it needs to do to be a new Emerald City. And Baltimore, which is struggling and has very limited resources—at least it has the port. Perhaps New Orleans is a different story in a way, because it's got tourism.

JONATHAN MACEY, *Professor of Corporate Law, Corporate Finance, and Securities Law, Yale Law School*: The problem is actually worse than you described it, because in discussions of localism versus regionalism, there seems to be this idea that if we can only get the wealthy outlying areas in a region to pitch in as they should, things would work well.

If you start with a political economy model in which politicians are rationally self-interested—and they don't want to invoke, encourage, or support policies that are going to increase the chances that they'll be marginalized, lose reelection, or become unimportant—then we have to at least entertain the possibility that in some context, the local politicians are also part of the problem. They don't want things like gentrification. They don't want things like Amazon moving into parts of New York.

I saw this a lot when I lived in Chicago on the South Side. Local politicians like Gus Savage and many others knew that gentrifying meant moving a lot of well-educated, wealthy people into the blighted areas they served, and that these new people may not support the incumbent, often corrupt politicians currently in power. Reform that would vastly improve the lives of these politicians' constituents likely would threaten the local politicians' hold on power.

We have this trend toward regionalism, which is great. I'm not sure that it's purely cheap, rich people blocking the trend—although there's certainly a great deal of that, and I'm not discounting it. There's also the problem on the demand side as well as the supply side.

SHAMBAUGH: If you ever have sat in on the Office of Information and Regulatory Affairs review of federal regulations, there is a massive amount of time that goes into the cost-benefit analysis for some of these rules. Then you realize states are passing almost exact parallel rules with no capacity to do that kind of analysis. It is a really important thing; we could have, frankly, a CBO-like thing for regulatory analysis that would basically be a consultant to states. That could help.

There was actually one model of this. I mentioned occupational licensing; we were really interested, in the Obama administration, but had no authority over it, because it's all at state level. They did stick something embarrassingly small [in the budget], like $7 million; you probably couldn't even find it in any budget table, because it's so small. That went to the National Conference of State Legislatures just to fund them doing the cost-benefit analysis for states that were thinking of redoing their occupational licensing.

There are models of ways to do this, but it's a really important point: For a lot of the things that we want states and cities to do efficiently, it's not fair to ask them to do the same type of stuff that the federal government can do.

LEVERE: There are networks. There are state policy priorities; therefore, there's budget and tax in virtually all the states. For our work, our goal is to reduce the waste of intellectual capital across all these communities by connecting these networks and sharing best practices. What is the next stage in that?

GERKEN: I know there are networks, but they're vastly outgunned—at least at the state level—by what's on the other side.

HACKER: There's a study by [political scientist] Alexander Hertel-Fernandez showing that roughly 1 percent of state laws are simply verbatim model legislation by ALEC, which seems low when you think about it, but 2 percent of all state legislation is essentially just written by a lobby organization. That's quite shocking. The states that have the highest rates aren't just Republican states; they're the ones that have the weakest legislative professionalism.

DAVID NEWVILLE, *VP for Policy and Research, Prosperity Now*: I want to echo a couple of comments that Jay made. The whole issue of leaving benefits on the table—for the EITC nationally, the uptake is around 80 percent. I don't know what it's like in certain localities; I'm sure it's lower. But SNAP take-up is [in the] low 50 percent [range]. There's been some pretty good research, at least in the EITC, that the money is spent in the community and gets reinvested there.

Finding these public-private partnerships to spread the word about these programs, like the Volunteer Income Tax Assistance sites I mentioned that are in every state in the country and many localities—these programs help folks file for their taxes and help people sign up for SNAP benefits while they're waiting to get their taxes done. They help people file. They make partnerships with larger employers; they can come and do taxes in the workplace, and encourage their employees to file. It's just another low-cost way of leveraging partnerships to get more money into the community, and that's important.

The other thing that was mentioned, the fines and fees issue, is a huge one. We're seeing a lot of movement around that across the country—also, at the state level, looking at driver's license suspensions, which is particularly painful for people when you think about getting to work. There's no public transportation. Your license is suspended. You lose your job. We know from the scarcity framework, just about low-income folks in general, that they can't manage all these things—show up to court, deal with these things. As much as you can take off their plate, to allow them to not have to deal with all this, could help low-income residents a lot.

There's one last thing I would say, and this would be Gene's expertise and others' more than mine. In general, [considering] what's going on at the national level with the Consumer Financial Protection Bureau and the regulatory level being out to lunch, probably for the next five years, [we're] really looking at wealth depletion and predatory practices at the city or state level among bad actors, particularly when it comes to discrimination. This will be important. And it's a good, even low-cost, way to help residents, because by removing some of these [local] predatory practices, which can be draining their pockets, you are making sure that they still have access to capital and other things, and [can] manage their finances. But taking off the worst actors, especially in terms of discrimination—it's important, even though it can be harder at the city and state levels to have the enforcement staff and the dollars there to do that. It'll be even more important for cities and states to pick that up in the future.

BRONIN: One thing unifies some of the themes that we've been talking about: the point that Gene made about both the skepticism and the prejudice that are often held toward struggling urban centers. The point—that skepticism and prejudice are often mutual—is actually a very important one, [and] it goes both directions. I don't think this is unique to Connecticut; this is a national issue. But it's particularly pronounced in Connecticut. When you have that kind of separation, it's not just psychological. In fact, it has very real economic consequences.

To this point just made about access to vehicles—40 percent of households in Hartford don't have access to a vehicle. About 85 percent of the jobs held [by people who live] in the city of Hartford are outside of the city of Hartford. An overwhelming majority of residents who work work outside the city.

One of the major constraints to accessing employment is the lack of access to transportation, and one of the things that helps create this sense of isolation and separation is the absence of a meaningful public transportation network. If you look at the public transit network that existed a century ago, it was this hub-and-spoke, train-and-trolley system that I'd give my left arm for right now. We may not replicate it just like that, but transportation investment could accomplish a lot of what we're talking about. The redistributive effect that Jacob [Hacker] talked about. The sense of common identity that Gene talked about, and the access to employment going both directions, is really important.

From a job-creation, job-generation standpoint, what's the modern version of the Civilian Conservation Corps? A stimulus focused on transportation could go a long way to combating much of what we talked about today—not to mention the environmental benefits of doing that.

BYRD: You made an interesting comment. A lot of people lost their lives or suffered during Hurricane Katrina because they didn't have transportation.

Financial literacy is huge in youth education, but parent education is huge. We're just getting ready to talk about getting low- and moderate-income people back into the banking system. I've been curious as to your thoughts—it's abusive to them to be outside a regulated system.

LUDWIG: You know better than I, Daryl. You've lived it.

Daryl is not unique, but he is really one of the top bankers of the United States in many ways—importantly, in the ways he personally embraces the needs of the communities his bank serves. He runs a successful, sizable institution that is incredibly civic by its own nature. It's remarkable, the degree to which Iberia plays a disproportionately significant role in the work that it does.

My sense, Daryl, is that you support CDFIs. They may be a big part of the solution nationally. As great a bank as IberiaBank is, it can't solve all the problems, even within its geographic footprint. There's work that I don't think even Iberia can do—nor can bigger, mainstream banks. They don't have the capacity to deal with it, and it's not economic for them. Only a CDFI can do that. CDFIs are closer to the ground than a big bank is.[60]

BYRD: What about the rules around small loans?

LUDWIG: Daryl, your comment about small loans goes to a potential flaw in the federal and state regulatory system. The system treats low- and moderate-income banking, including banking by CDFIs, the same way. And we all know that in a variety of ways, CDFIs are different— they are devoted to service and mission more than to shareholder return. Moreover, their products are fundamentally tailored to help lower-income Americans succeed. I do not think in this case a one-size-fits-all regulatory process makes sense. Regulation needs to be tailored to this unique group of companies in ways that maintain safety and soundness but reflect the need to accommodate their mission-driven status.

This same concern for regulations tailored to mission-driven institutions should be equally applicable to mission-driven products. For example, "refund anticipation" loans have been given a bad name. They are loans that provide immediate funding and services for low-income Americans to file and receive their money for low-income tax benefits. To date, regulations have punished banks in this business because of the high APRs that can be calculated from the activity. Indeed, charges may be too high in some instances. But this is an activity that can add value. Creating regulations that recognize this as a mission-driven function that can add value to low- and moderate-income Americans should be specially treated so that the service can be provided at fair rates.

MACEY: On the point about noncompete clauses and similar sorts of things, it raises—without expressing my own views—the question, why do we observe these things? One hypothesis, which seems to be the hypothesis embraced in this room by everyone except me, is if we could just sit down in the room with these policymakers or regulators about governance, they would understand the technical information we're giving them, and regulation would be sensible.

LUDWIG: When Sarah [Bloom Raskin] was in office, we dealt with this problem of trying to repay the Troubled Asset Relief Program (TARP). If it wasn't for Sarah, the CDFIs and many of the banks that predominantly serve African American communities would have been hung out to dry. But even with Sarah's help, much remains to be done. Approximately 50 percent of them got TARP repayment options that made sense, but approximately 50 percent are still hanging out to dry because there has been inadequate political courage to rectify this situation.[61]

MACEY: What I object to is this notion that somehow these people who are the policymakers or people in power are not doing the right thing because they don't have the right technical information, as opposed to not doing the right thing because it's in their own private interest [not] to do so.

LUDWIG: You have Sarah. You have Luke [Bronin]. You have young people around this room who really are people with backbone. They're working hard. Some folks who should be here, need to be here, are down in Georgia enjoying the Masters [Golf Tournament]. I know it. Now, doesn't that say a little something about the need to change the narrative in our country? My comment goes too often to many of the folks we end up electing to government—the folks who are supposedly leading. We've got some real stars around the table and in the government who are dedicated to this mission. But we have fewer civic-minded Americans than we need right now.

GERKEN: I want to say the last word if you don't mind, Gene. You may not know that yesterday was Gene's birthday. We owe thanks to the staff. But we all especially owe thanks to Gene. This is an exceedingly odd way to spend the twenty-four hours of your birthday, but for all of us, it was a gift. And I just want to say: Thank you very much.

A Call to Action

Several weeks after the conference in New Haven, I had occasion to drive up from Washington, D.C., to Baltimore, Maryland. Nearing my destination, I passed through one of this troubled city's poorer neighborhoods. I remembered the neighborhood well, having once been enrolled at the Peabody Institute, located just blocks away.[62] During my student days, the neighborhood had been defined by its proud and beautiful townhouses. Today, by contrast, these structures are decaying away, which made me feel a bit like I was visiting a Roman ruin. Worse still was the human tragedy on display—the homelessness, the drug refuse, the beleaguered "convenience" stores.

When a traffic light turned red at a relatively desolate intersection, two young men on the curb stood up, smiled at me, waved, and offered to clean my windshield. They were young, handsome, and clearly industrious. My sense, just from a quick glance, was that they had most everything any employer would want if a nearby business was hiring. And I could envision how giving these young men an opportunity to do something beyond cleaning windshields would redound both to society's broader benefit and to their own. But I fear, given America's current trajectory, those sorts of opportunities remain elusive for them. It's a human tragedy that should bring tears to our eyes, spurring the public and private sectors alike to do better.

That very brief interaction got me thinking about a whole range of topics—many of which tracked back to the conference in New Haven. I couldn't help but notice how the two men standing outside my car lived in circumstances so different from my own. How opportunity flows from circumstance. How blessed I am by the privileges I've been afforded through the whole of my life. And how frustrating it must be to live in a community bedeviled by dead ends. Even as pundits and analysts talk about the American economy as though it's never been better, for huge swaths of poor, working, and middle-class America, life since the Great Recession has been far short of miraculous.

However others might have judged them—whatever prejudice might have reared its ugly head—one thing was undeniable. The two young men offering to clean my windshield were working hard, jumping off the curb each time the light turned red to see if they could convert a customer. If their toil was earning them anything approaching minimum wage, I'd be surprised. No doubt some of drivers they approach reacted stone-faced, or with unfriendly grimaces. But they were keeping at it, nothing if not determined. They were clearly eager to perform a service. Imagine for a moment how the economy might grow if men and women with the imperturbable tenacity of these two young men were employed by any of the companies throughout the United States that are desperate for new labor, and yet can't seem to find qualified workers to hire.

Whether in Baltimore, York, Albany, or Flint—whether in urban, suburban, or rural communities—what we can't ever forget is that middle- and working-class Americans have struggled and are struggling, even through the longest peacetime economic expansion in America's history. The reasons vary from person to person and from community to community. Some people are the victims of prejudice and legacy discrimination. Others are simply too far from centers of contemporary commerce. Some may lack the will to thrive in the twenty-first-century economy—but many more simply lack the necessary skills and any semblance of opportunity. And the end result is the same: They suffer amid plenty.

If nothing else emerged from our conversation at Yale Law School—and a great deal certainly did—it was a broad recognition that any happy talk about the state of America's economy ignores the underlying reality for so many Americans. I doubt anyone left the gathering anything but more determined to do something to fix that fundamental injustice.

The questions of *why* we face this reality and *what* we ought to do about it received a great deal of attention, and the various and competing theories and strategies all have a great deal to recommend them. The scholarship and expertise on display in those sitting around the table guaranteed that the ideas were well researched and of high quality, if not universally accepted. And the discussion provided ample opportunity for participants to sharpen their thinking and incorporate new wrinkles and theories into their own explanations and proposals.

To my hearing, a few points deserve particular mention.

First, to say it again, our measurements of the economy are an ever-present disaster. We simply don't have a good way of quantifying, even as late as 2019, what's happening to the nation's middle and working classes. That has frequently prompted policymakers to focus on the wrong challenges. No one at the conference disagreed with the central premise: America needs better standards when measuring the economy. Anyone reading this should view that reality as a central takeaway.

Second, the challenges facing middle- and working-class Americans cannot be resolved exclusively by the public sector. As many around the table agreed, the private sector has a crucial role to play—and they should do so without government having to hold their feet to the fire.

Jonathan Tepper's recent book, *The Myth of Capitalism*, argues that disparities of opportunity are, to an important degree, the result of monopolistic and oligopolistic behavior among various private enterprises. When power is too concentrated—as it was at the zenith of the Roman Empire, during the age of the American robber barons, and at fraught moments in world history before and after—productivity suffers, and inequality is almost invariably exacerbated. That may well be happening now, yet again.

The good news is that whatever anyone thinks of the work being done in Washington—and few think much of Congress's progress at the moment—the private sector has begun to understand that the ball is at least partly in their court. The Business Roundtable's statement calling for executives to think beyond quarterly earnings reports was an important step. Insofar as the working and middle classes are suffering in 2019, productivity will eventually begin to flag, and broad inequality will sow doubts about the underlying value of free enterprise. That's an outcome business leaders want to avoid.

Finally, there is this: It would be a shame if the discussions at Yale were not viewed as a call to action. It was, of course, gratifying to have so many prolific scholars and practitioners around the table, and to have such an august roster of participants. But unless the best among our ideas eventually weave their way into broader public discourse, our ultimate aims will have been left unfulfilled. Time is of the essence. And on this point, history serves as a guide.

When a society's working and middle classes are trapped without opportunity for a sustained period of time, the results are rarely pretty. Whether or not you buy the premise of economic determinism, stagnation and inequality almost certainly play a role in fomenting war and bloodshed. World War II was just the latest global, tragic example. The German middle class, haunted by a sense that their well-being was in interminable decline, were urged to rise up, take over the government, and establish a new totalitarian order—which, at Hitler's behest, they did.

It wasn't just economics, of course. But economic realities born from the Versailles Treaty that had ended World War I played a crucial role. And while we may not be on the *immediate* precipice of something so ghastly, none of us can know with complete certainty what the future has in store.

If this conference represented a step toward providing America's leaders with an understanding of how to react to the underlying reality facing large but forgotten portions of the population, then perhaps our next challenge is to build the political coalition that will help champion the best among the proposed solutions. What these pages offer is a down payment on the massive shift we need to effectuate. The challenges we face in the twenty-first century are not exactly the same as those previous generations of Americans have overcome. But the need for resolve has not changed.

To steal a phrase: History does not repeat itself, but it rhymes. We should endeavor, together, to ensure the future tracks a different, more prosperous path for poor, working-, and middle-class Americans. And we should begin now, because before long, efforts on this front may prove too late.

Acknowledgments

Much as my career has primarily spanned the worlds of law and banking, my life's work is largely reflected in the substance of this book. From a young age, my family impressed upon me the importance of addressing the inequities that plague American society across a range of dimensions. Market capitalism and the free enterprise system may stand alone as the most effective means of creating prosperity, but there was no way to be raised in York, Pennsylvania, two generations ago—or to drive by the homeless encampments situated today outside the Federal Reserve Board in Washington, D.C.—without realizing that the prevailing economy doesn't work for too many Americans. I was raised to believe that it's everyone's responsibility to be part of the solution.

Years ago, at the beginning of my career in public service, a well-respected economist took me aside and explained, "Gene, at the end of the day, people are poor for a reason." I knew what he was trying to tell me, and but for the way I was raised in York, I might not have realized that he was full of nonsense. His insinuation that poverty is inbred—that those living with less deserve to endure their circumstances—is utterly preposterous. This conference at Yale proves the point. So while I can't list them all, I want to acknowledge all the people who have helped me, through my more than seven decades, to appreciate that truth and to never forget it.

In America, if not around the world, everyone deserves a chance to make the most of their innate abilities. The hard reality is that our system today too frequently squanders the potential of our people. But if you give those who need it a hand up, many can take it and do great things. If we don't champion the programs and policies that provide opportunity, it will not just be the poor who sink.

I want to offer special thanks to our symposium co-host, Dean Heather Gerken, and the Yale Law economics and political science faculty, including Jacob Hacker, Jonathan Macey, Daniel Markovits, Zachary Liscow, Anika Singh Lemar, and Robert Shiller, along with our other distinguished symposium participants: Oren Cass, Steven Pearlstein, Andrea Levere, Sarah Bloom Raskin, Larry Summers, Glenn Hubbard, Andrew Tisch, Mary Skafidas, Isabel Sawhill, Luke Bronin, Jay Shambaugh, Daryl Byrd, Mary Miller, Michael Moskow, Deval Patrick, Susan Krause Bell, David Newville, and Jim Millstein who were of course critical to this book coming together. Thank you all for your wisdom, insights, edits, and commentary.

The staff of both the Yale Law School and the Ludwig Institute for Shared Economic Prosperity (LISEP) were crucial to pulling off the event smoothly, and then translating its contents to this volume. Thanks go to Stephanie Allen and Marc Dunkelman for their editing and research, Brai Odion-Esene and Philip Kalikman for their research assistance, and Pamela Watson, Courtney Stockland, and Rebecca Yochum for their organizational prowess. Thanks also to Yale's Laura Lauro and Sara Lulo for all of their assistance. My appreciation to Kris Pauls and her staff at Disruption Books for understanding how critical this topic is and for bringing this project to life.

Thanks to Michael Levy, Steve Harris, Chairman Don Riegle, Vernon Jordan, and Jan Piercy for their thoughtful comments regarding the seminar and the premises for the book. My appreciation also to the members of the Promontory Advisory Board who serve as a constant sounding board: Mary Schapiro, Frank Zarb, Morris Offit, Mark Jacobsen, Alfred Moses,

Gene McQuade, Ken Duberstein, Jeffrey Goldstein, Arthur Levitt, Richard Ketchum, and Barry Zubrow. Thanks as well to Sarah Diamond and Bridget van Kralingen for their thoughtfulness and encouragement.

Most important, I want to express my appreciation to my wife, Carol, and our family, including my brother Ken, for their patience, encouragement, and wisdom through my decades-long obsession with the plight of America's poor, working, and middle classes. I'm quite sure that, through the years, they have heard more about these topics from me than they might have preferred. But they've rarely responded with anything but love, good humor, and insightful ideas. I am forever in their debt.

Notes

1   See my brother Ken Ludwig's play, "Dear Jack, Dear Louise," for an artist's view of my parents during WWII.

2   Jeremy Hobson, "Philadelphia, Pittsburgh and Alabama in Between? Not Really," on *Here & Now*, podcast, WBUR, April 26, 2016, https://www.wbur.org /hereandnow/2016/04/26/diverse-philadelphia-politics.

3   "School Lunch—Students Eligible for Free or Reduced-Price Lunch in York," Hanover Public (Suburban), May 2018, https://datacenter.kidscount.org/data/tables/2720 -school-lunch--students-eligible-for-free-or-reduced-price-lunch?loc=40&loct=10#detai led/10/5659/false/1639,1600,1536,1460,1249,1120,1024,937,809,712 /any/10324,10325.

4   York County Office of Communications, "Our Response to the Heroin Epidemic," York County Pennsylvania, https://yorkcountypa.gov/communications-office/the-heroin -epidemic-in-york-county.html.

5   Gordon Rago, "'Worst Year,' 'Terrifying Trend' Define Opioids in 2017," *York Daily Record*, January 8, 2018, https://www.ydr.com/story/news/crime/2018/01/05/worst-year -terrifying-trend-opioid-heroin-deaths-17-ravage-central-pa-counties/1004495001/.

6   Todd Spangler, "The Rust Belt Gave Trump Victory, Now They Want Jobs in Return," *Detroit Free Press*, January 18, 2017, https://www.usatoday.com/story/news /politics/2017/01/18/rust-belt-voters-donald-trump/96670922/.

7   "US Business Cycle Expansions and Contractions," National Bureau of Economic Research, https://www.nber.org/cycles/cyclesmain.html.

8   Rebecca Ungarino, "US Stocks Surge to a Record Close After Trump and Xi's Trade-War Truce," Markets Insider, July 1, 2019, https://markets.businessinsider.com/news/stocks /us-stock-market-record-trump-xi-g20-trade-war-truce-2019-7-1028322208?utm _source=markets&utm_medium=ingest.

9   Bureau of Labor Statistics, "Databases, Tables & Calculators by Subject," US Department of Labor, https://data.bls.gov/timeseries/LNS14000000.

10 "Executive Paywatch," AFL-CIO, https://aflcio.org/paywatch.

11   "Report on the Economic Well-Being of U.S. Households in 2018," Board of Governors of the Federal Reserve System, May 2019, https://www.federalreserve.gov/publications/2019 -economic-well-being-of-us-households-in-2018-higher-education.htm.

12   Enrico Moretti, "The New Geography of Jobs," Federal Reserve Bank of San Francisco, https://www.frbsf.org/education/files/Transcript_Moretti_The-New-Geography-of-Jobs.pdf.

13   "Distribution of Household Wealth in the U.S. since 1989," Board of Governors of the Federal Reserve System, September 27, 2019, https://www.federalreserve.gov/releases/z1 /dataviz/dfa/distribute/chart/.

14   US Bureau of Labor Statistics, "Employment-Population Ratio," US Department of Labor, September 15, 2019, https://www.bls.gov/charts/employment-situation /employment-population-ratio.htm.

15   "Labour Force Participation Rate," OECD Employment Outlook, https://data.oecd.org /emp/labour-force-participation-rate.htm.

16   "Report on the Economic Well-Being of U.S. Households in 2018 – May 2019," Board of Governors of the Federal Reserve System, https://www.federalreserve.gov/publications/2019 -economic-well-being-of-us-households-in-2018-dealing-with-unexpected-expenses.htm.

17   2019 Prosperity Now Scorecard, Prosperity Now, https://scorecard.prosperitynow.org /data-by-issue#finance/localoutcome/liquid-asset-poverty-rate.

18   "America's Shrinking Middle Class: A Closer Look at Changes Within Metropolitan Areas," Pew Research Center, May 11, 2016, https://www.pewsocialtrends.org/2016 /05/11/americas-shrinking-middle-class-a-close-look-at-changes-within-metropolitan -areas/.

19   Ibid.

20   David Pilling, "Five Ways GDP Gets It Wrong as a Measure of Our Success," World Economic Forum, January 17, 2018, https://www.weforum.org/agenda/2018/01/gdp -frog-matchbox-david-pilling-growth-delusion/.

21   Ibid.

22   "Employment: Time Spent in Paid and Unpaid Work, by Sex," OECD, https://stats .oecd.org/index.aspx?queryid=54757.

23   Bureau of Labor Statistics, "Employment-Population Ratio," US Department of Labor, September 15, 2019, https://www.bls.gov/charts/employment-situation/employment -population-ratio.htm.

24   Ilana Boivie, "Pensionomics 2018: Measuring the Economic Impact of Defined Benefit Pension Expenditures," National Institute on Retirement Security, January 2019, https://www.nirsonline.org/reports/pensionomics-2018-measuring-the-economic -impact-of-defined-benefit-pension-expenditures/.

25   Dan Kopf, "If U.S. Unemployment Rate Included Everyone Who Says They Want a Job, It Would Be Nearly Double," Quartz, January 5, 2017, https://qz.com/877432/the -us-unemployment-rate-measure-is-deceptive-and-doesnt-need-to-be/.

26   "Missing Workers—The Missing Part of the Unemployment Story," Economic Policy Institute, July 7, 2017, https://www.epi.org/publication/missing-workers/.

27   "Financing Baltimore's Growth: Strengthening Lending to Small Businesses," John Hopkins 21st Century Cities Initiative, August 2018, http://21cc.jhu.edu/publications /reports/financing-baltimores-growth-strengthening-lending-to-small-businesses/.

28   William Lazonick, Philip Moss, Hal Salzman, and Öner Tulum, "Skill Development and Sustainable Prosperity: Cumulative and Collective Careers versus Skill-Biased Technical Change," page 5, Institute for New Economic Thinking, December 8, 2014, https:// www.ineteconomics.org/uploads/papers/Skill-Development-and-Sustainable -Prosperity-20141208.pdf.

29   "Median Usual Weekly Nominal Earnings, High School Graduate (Year-over-Year Percentage Change)—No College," St. Louis Fed FRED Database, January 17, 2019, https://fred.stlouisfed.org/series/LEU0252921300A.

30   Ibid.

31   Isabel Sawhill, "What the Forgotten Americans Really Want—and How to Give It to Them," Brooking Institute, October 2018, https://www.brookings.edu/longform/what -the-forgotten-americans-really-want-and-how-to-give-it-to-them/.

32   William C. Dunkelberg and Holly Wade, "NFIB Small Business Economic Trends," NFIB Research Center, July 2019, https://www.nfib.com/assets/SBET-July-2019-PDF.pdf.

33   Bureau of Labor Statistics, "Economic News Release, Job Openings and Labor Turnover," US Department of Labor, July 5, 2019, https://www.bls.gov/news.release/jolts.nr0.htm.

34   Craig A. Giffi, Paul Wellener, and Ben Dollar, "The Jobs Are Here but Where Are the People?," Deloitte, November 14, 2018, https://www2.deloitte.com/insights/us/en /industry/manufacturing/manufacturing-skills-gap-study.html.

35   "Losing Our Minds: Brain Drain Across the United States," US Congress Joint Economic Community, April 24, 2019, https://www.jec.senate.gov/public/index.cfm /republicans/2019/4/losing-our-minds-brain-drain-across-the-united-states#_edn1.

36   Matt Vasilogambros, "Midwest a Victim of 'Rural Brain Drain,'" HuffPost, updated May 25, 2011, https://www.huffpost.com/entry/rural-brain-drain-iowa_b_830352 ?guccounter=1&guce_referrer=aHR0cHM6Ly9zZWFyY2gueWFob28uY29tLw&guce _referrer_sig=AQAAAAeFXYQ3rFbLm3CsWEzkdF83UrgorfC-lvQhms6d7dnz9Rlxsiz Qb8l7JfR8kl9NIGAYxfkoV-83Gv8ux7iT3m77JcFKVTXy6lin9D0ZeD7SAKKGEVHy scXrdkYpLshlVMlzch4Xz8kgHsOESWZ6Mn3Gk4cB7WzWqf4Q_msw8TRt.

37   2019 Prosperity Now Scorecard, Prosperity Now, https://scorecard.prosperitynow.org /data-by-issue#finance/localoutcome/liquid-asset-poverty-rate.

38   Alicia Adamczyk, "Full-Time Minimum Wage Workers Cannot Afford a 2-Bedroom Rental Anywhere in the US," CNBC, June 26, 2019, https://www.cnbc.com/2019/06 /26/minimum-wage-workers-cannot-afford-2-bedroom-rental-anywhere-in-the-us.html.

39   "The State of the Nation's Housing Report 2019," Joint Center for Housing Studies of Harvard University, July 1, 2019, https://www.jchs.harvard.edu/sites/default/files /Harvard_JCHS_State_of_the_Nations_Housing_2019.pdf.

40   "Renters Report Housing Costs Significantly Impact Their Health Care," Enterprise Community Partners, April 3, 2019, https://www.enterprisecommunity.org/news-and -events/news-releases/2019-04_renters-report-housing-costs-significantly-impact-their -health-care.

41   Briana Boyington and Emma Kerr, "20 Years of Tuition Growth at National
     Universities," *U.S. News*, September 19, 2019, https://www.usnews.com/education/best
     -colleges/paying-for-college/articles/2017-09-20/see-20-years-of-tuition-growth-at
     -national-universities.

42   James McBride, "The State of U.S. Infrastructure," Council on Foreign Relations,
     January 12, 2018, https://www.cfr.org/backgrounder/state-us-infrastructure.

43   "Household Debt Continues to Climb in Third Quarter as Mortgage and Auto Loan
     Originations Grow," Federal Reserve Bank of New York, November 13, 2019,
     https://www.newyorkfed.org/newsevents/news/research/2019/20191113.

44   Patrick McLaughlin and Laura Stanley, "Regulation and Income Inequality: The
     Regressive Effects of Entry Regulations," Mercatus Center at George Mason University,
     January 20, 2016, https://www.mercatus.org/publication/regulation-and-income
     -inequality-regressive-effects-entry-regulations-0.

45   Bureau of Labor Statistics, "Projections of Occupational Employment, 2016–26," US
     Department of Labor, October 2017, https://www.bls.gov/careeroutlook/2017/article
     /occupational-projections-charts.htm#growth-in-occupations-by-education-typically
     -required.

46   Austan Goolsbee and Glenn Hubbard, "A Policy Agenda to Develop Human Capital for the
     Modern Economy," The Aspen Institute, February 4, 2019, https://www.aspeninstitute.org
     /longform/expanding-economic-opportunity-for-more-americans/a-policy-agenda-to
     -develop-human-capital-for-the-modern-economy/.

47   Tess C. Taylor, "The Costs of Training New Employees, Including Hidden Expenses,"
     ADP, October 15, 2018, https://www.adp.com/spark/articles/2018/10/the-costs-of
     -training-new-employees-including-hidden-expenses.aspx.

48   Eugene Ludwig, "Payroll Tax Has Become a Monster; It Needs to Be Replaced,"
     Newsweek, July 11, 2019, https://www.newsweek.com/payroll-tax-monster-needs
     -replacing-2020-1448767.

49   Eugene Ludwig, "The Key to Rightsizing Regulation," *American Banker*, June 20, 2019,
     https://www.americanbanker.com/opinion/the-key-to-rightsizing-regulation.

50   Boston Redevelopment Authority, Zoning Code, Article 37 – Green Building, https://
     library.municode.com/ma/boston/codes/redevelopment_authority?nodeId=ART37GRBU.

51   Timothy Weaver, "The Problem with Opportunity Zones," CityLab, May 16, 2018,
     https://www.citylab.com/equity/2018/05/the-problem-with-opportunity-zones/560510/.

52   "New York Homelessness Statistics," United States Interagency Council on
     Homelessness, https://www.usich.gov/homelessness-statistics/ny.

53   "Criminal Justice Factsheet," NAACP, https://www.naacp.org/criminal-justice-fact-sheet/.

54   Melissa S. Kearney et al., "Ten Economic Facts About Crime and Incarceration in the
     United States," The Hamilton Project, May 2014, https://www.hamiltonproject.org
     /assets/legacy/files/downloads_and_links/v8_THP_10CrimeFacts.pdf.

55   Emily Badger, "Whites Have Huge Wealth Edge over Blacks (but Don't Know It)," *New
     York Times*, September 18, 2017, https://www.nytimes.com/interactive/2017/09/18
     /upshot/black-white-wealth-gap-perceptions.html.

56   "Total Household Debt Climbs for 20th Straight Quarter as Mortgage Debt and
      Originations Rise," Federal Reserve Bank of New York, Q2 2019, https://www
      .newyorkfed.org/newsevents/news/research/2019/20190813.

57   Aimee Picchi, "America's Job Problem: Low-Wage Work Is Growing Fastest," CBS News,
      August 4, 2017, https://www.cbsnews.com/news/americas-job-problem-low-wage-work
      -is-growing-fastest/.

58   James R. Barth, Tong Liy, and Wenling Lu, "Banking Regulation in the United States,"
      CESifo Economic Studies, 2009, http://webhome.auburn.edu/~barthjr/publications/Bank
      percent20Regulation percent20in percent20the percent20United percent20States.pdf.

59   "Income and Wealth in the United States: An Overview of Recent Data," The Peter G.
      Peterson Foundation, October 4, 2019, https://www.pgpf.org/blog/2019/10/income
      -and-wealth-in-the-united-states-an-overview-of-data.

60   Elise Balboni and Christina Travers, "CDFIs & Impact Investing: An Industry Review,"
      The Federal Reserve Bank of New York, December 2017, https://www.newyorkfed.org
      /medialibrary/media/outreach-and-education/2017/CDFIs-Impact-Investing.pdf.

61   Trymaine Lee, "Black-Owned Banks Struggle to Stay Out of the Red," HuffPost,
      August 22, 2011, https://www.huffpost.com/entry/black-owned-banks
      -struggl_n_933216.

62   The Peabody Institute is a wonderful school of music, but I did more for American
      music's future successes by leaving Peabody than if I'd stayed on and tried to pretend
      music prowess.

Index

About the Editor

GENE LUDWIG is the founder of the Promontory family of companies and Canapi LLC, the largest financial technology venture fund in the United States. He is the CEO of Promontory Financial Group, an IBM company, and chairman of Promontory MortgagePath, a technology-based mortgage fulfillment and solutions company. He is the former vice chairman and senior control officer of Bankers Trust New York Corp, served as the United States comptroller of the currency from 1993 to 1998 under President Bill Clinton, and was a partner at Covington & Burling from 1981 to 1992.

In 2019, The Ludwig Family Foundation, a 501(c)(3) organization founded by Mr. Ludwig and his wife, Dr. Carol Ludwig, created a new program, The Ludwig Institute for Shared Economic Prosperity (LISEP), dedicated to improving the economic well-being of lower-income Americans through research and education. The LISEP program is focused on better understanding and disseminating relevant data and policy recommendations intended to expand meaningful, high-wage opportunities for such individuals.

His writing has appeared in *The Financial Times, The New York Times, The Wall Street Journal, American Banker,* and *Time.* His 2008 *WSJ* op ed with Paul Volcker and Nicholas Brady, along with other financial crisis commentary, is credited with helping to avoid greater disaster.

He holds a master's degree from Oxford University and is a New College Oxford fellow. He holds a JD from Yale University, where he was editor of the *Yale Law Journal* and chairman of Yale Legislative Services.

Gene lives in Washington, D.C., with his wife, Dr. Carol Ludwig. They have three children and two dogs who run the household.